Once Upon An Eternity

by David Edman

For Charles Scott
— w/ warmest
regards + great
esteem —

David
8-9-84

Book design, illustrations, layout and mechanicals
by Dave Titus
Typography by Sandra Ramirez-Guerrero
Cover photograph courtesy of Meade Instruments Corpora-
tion, Costa Mesa, CA

Table of Contents

CHAPTER 1
Fireworks

The Banquet was interrupted briefly for fireworks.

Trazel, who had recently been created, saw flashes of light and heard explosions. Immediately he rushed to the nearest parapet and there stared wide-eyed at the splendor of it all.

The fireworks seemed to have their origin in the vicinity of the Head Table. They appeared initially as globules of liquid light. Then, floating off toward the Circle of Becoming, this side of the Everlasting Darkness, they suddenly exploded into showers of incandescent fragments.

With each explosion came audible expressions of pleasure from those at the Banquet. A few cheers were raised here and there, and these encouraged Trazel to dance about and do some cheering of his own.

Karam-Bor, who'd been given charge of Trazel, recognized the voice, and came dashing to the foot of the parapet steps looking decidedly out of sorts. His latest novice, he'd discovered, had a way of going off on his own, and Karam-Bor did not appreciate it at all.

"Well, *here* you are!" he said in a way which implied that Trazel was where Trazel ought not to be.

"Karam-Bor, come look! Come see the fireworks, and tell me you've never, never, never seen anything half so exciting!"

Karam-Bor mounted the parapet with his usual dignity and cast a critical eye on the spectacle.

"Well, if you must know," he said. "I've seen as good. Many times!"

"You mean He does this often?"

"Whenever it suits Him."

"How marvelous! How perfectly marvelous!" Trazel sighed.

"Marvelous? I suppose so. I wouldn't go so far as to deny it. But it's not all show either. Each one of those enormous bangs out there marks an invasion of the darkness. And you know what that means!"

"I ... I'm not sure I do."

"It means *work!* It means *follow-up!* It means assignments for the likes of you and me. After all, you just don't go pushing back the borders of darkness without attending to the details, as you'll find out soon enough."

"It's still utterly marvelous!"

"That," said Karam-Bor, "is what the new ones always say."

Trazel was not the least crushed by Karam-Bor's detachment, for he was still entranced by the billions upon billions of light fragments as they eddied and swirled toward a relentless blackness.

After awhile he said, "Where do they go, Karam-Bor — all those bits of light?"

"They keep passing through the Circle of Becoming until they reach the borders of the Everlasting Darkness."

"What happens then?"

"There are those assigned to sweep up what remains."

"Is anything lost?"

"Oh, a little, I should imagine. But there is more gain than loss."

"But that little that may be lost — what happens to it?"

"It gets swallowed up by the Everlasting Darkness, or so I'm told."

"Does that mean it's gone forever?"

"I'm sure I don't know," said Karam-Bor with some impatience. "What concerns me at the moment is that your *questions* will go on forever."

A pensive look came over Trazel's face. But this soon became overtaken by a mischievous look. All of a sudden he whirled round, leaned backward over the parapet, and gazed out at the fireworks upside down.

Karam-Bor clicked his disapproval.

"Karam-Bor! That space all around us. I mean, out there where the lights are swirling, swirling. Why is it called the Circle of Becoming?"

"Adopt a respectable position and I'll tell you."

Trazel straightened, and made an exaggerated effort at utter solemnity.

"All right, that's better," Karam-Bor said. "Now to your question. You want to know why that area out there is called the Circle of Becoming. The answer is this. Attend carefully. It is called the Circle of Becoming because it is neither complete light, nor total darkness. It is, you might say, neither reality nor unreality. Admittedly it does have various potentialities. I mean with regard to either. That is the answer to your question. Do you understand?"

"Of course I do," said Trazel, looking a bit dazed. "Though, to put it another way, not completely. I do and I don't. What I mean is, yes. That is to a point. But ... no to a point too." This was followed by a deep sigh, and: "I guess I'll have to admit, Karam-Bor, I'm not nearly so wise as you."

"Well," said Karam-Bor, softening. "Remember that one of the first signs of wisdom is the ability to recognize one's own ignorance. So mind what I'm saying. What I'm trying to tell you is that the C. of B. — by which I mean the Circle of Becoming — the C. of B. has certain metaphysical and ontological propensities. Surely you understand that!"

"Oh my yes! That makes it really simple," said Trazel, stifling a titter.

Karam-Bor, suspecting that he was being trifled with, turned to go.

"Oh, but what I don't understand is whether *He* rules out there or not," said Trazel quickly.

Karam-Bor stopped. The question was one on which he had definite opinions.

"Well, yes and no," he said. "Where there is pure light, there His laws are sovereign. Where you find pure darkness, there is ... nothing."

"Nothing?"

"Nothing. ... Oh, maybe a little chaos around the edges. A little disorder. But what it all comes to in the end is nothing."

"The Lord of Darkness is nothing?"

"He's well on the way."

"Then what about those places where there is both light and darkness?"

"A mishmash, essentially. Happiness. Tears. Fortune. Accident. Awakening. Dying. A little of this, a little of that."

"So complicated," said Trazel.

"You'll get the hang of it before long."

Trazel could think of nothing to say. In the ensuing silence he noted that there had come also a brief lull in the display of fireworks. There came now the sounds of banqueting in the Great Hall — the chink of dishes, the languid buzz of conversation, the occasional stirrings of laughter.

It raised within the youthful novice a new train of thought.

"Karam-Bor," he asked. "Is it true that those at the Banquet came from the Circle of Becoming?"

"It is indeed."

"How so?"

Karam-Bor shrugged.

"They chose to come."

"Just chose? Nothing more?"

"Absolutely nothing. He issued the invitation. They accepted."

"There must be more to it than that!"

"I assure you, there is not," Karam-Bor declared. "He simply let them know about the Banquet. The rest was up to them."

"With all His power and paraphernalia, I suppose it would be difficult to refuse."

"He doesn't lay it on, if that's what you're thinking. Anyway, I think I've had enough questions for now."

"Oh, just a few more, Karam-Bor! Please! I have some really teeny-tiny questions I've been wondering about ever so long! And I *know* you have the answers."

Karam-Bor drew himself up.

"Well, I'll do my best."

"Oh thanks. I knew you would. So here's the first. Tell me, why is there an Everlasting Darkness at all?"

"Mmmmmm. ... Why is there an Everlasting Darkness at all? Now that's an extremely complex question."

"Of course you could turn it around and tell me why there is a Kingdom of Light!"

"Yes, I could at that. But then, it requires certain conjectures of an etiological nature — "

"Or why is there a Lord of Light?"

"Ah, but there you're bound to begin with various preliminary hypotheses — "

"Or tell me this, Karam-Bor! Why is there anything at *all?*"

"Anything at all?"

"Yes, anything at all! Why is there *something,* not *nothing?*"

"Oh, that's a *ridiculous* question! You're just peddling *nonsense,* Trazel! Really, I'm fresh out of patience! You young ones simply *froth* with questions! And you're the worst I've ever known! Honestly, I do hope the next time they give me someone a little less frisky!"

"But it's all so curious, Karam-Bor! You've got to wonder! And yet — " Trazel paused, then suddenly whirled himself about in an utterly uninhibited pirouette, "it's all so wonderful too!"

At this moment, yet another blob of pure light floated serenely overhead on its way to the Circle of Becoming. Then, with a thunderclap that shook the battlements on which they stood, it fragmented into a dazzle of diamonds.

"Hooray! Hooray!" shouted Trazel. "Encore! Encore! Serve up another one! Another one!"

"I would beg you to *control* yourself, Trazel!" said Karam-Bor, scandalized to the very center of his being. "Remember who ... whom it is you're talking to!"

"But Karam-Bor, I can't help it!"

"Yes you *can* help it," said Karam-Bor hissing slightly. "And the best way to do that is to get busy. After all, that's why we're here, in case you've forgotten. To help out. To work. So let's be on our way, or we'll be late. ..."

Trazel walked dutifully down the parapet steps. It wasn't until he reached the bottom that the implication of the words struck him. He stopped in his tracks.

"Late?" he repeated softly. "Late for what?"

"Our appointment."

"Appointment? Do you mean — "

"I do. We're to be given an assignment."

"For sure?"

"Now why would I be saying a thing if it weren't so?"

"But where, Karam-Bor?"

"Somewhere out there."

"In the Circle of Becoming?"

"That's the place."

"But where in the Circle of Becoming? Where?"

"I don't know myself. But we'll find out soon enough. In

the meantime, may I advise you to start behaving a bit more like someone who's about to receive a serious responsibility?"

CHAPTER 2
A Stroll Beside The Great Hall

The avenue along which they now began to direct their steps possessed a rich burnished luster. Trees lined either side. Underneath lay broad green lawns sculptured with flower beds and pools, hedges, shrubs and fountains.

Park benches were situated everywhere, occupied for the most part by those who had taken a recess from the Banquet. Trazel observed some engaged in deep conversation. Others appeared to be trading jests. Still others seemed quite content with their own company — reading, humming, jotting down ideas, sketching, or just staring out into space, as though in the process of creating couplets or polishing a flight of melody.

Near one particular fountain a reunion of some sort seemed to be taking place. Trazel watched as a newcomer, who appeared a bit bewildered, submitted to ever so many embraces and cries of welcome.

An immense facade of glass, a wall of the Great Hall, paralleled the avenue. This wall stretched from the battlements near the Head Table as far as the eye could see.

The two began their stroll down the avenue sedately enough. Trazel seemed content to walk decorously at Karam-Bor's side, observing the sights all around him, for he was still fairly new on the scene and filled with considerable curiosity.

From what he could see of the Banquet through the glass, it seemed a rather informal affair. The revelers partook of a vast array of cuisine which came from kitchens on enormous round trays held aloft by servers with an uncanny sense of balance. Nor was there any shortage of wine, for great crystal decanters crowded the tables — some filled with a wine that was blood red in color, others possessing a tawny cast, while still others held a perfect clarity.

For all the variety and richness of fare, the banqueters did not appear so hungry or thirsty that they neglected one another. The affair seemed as much a feast of conversation as it was of food and wine. And those who wearied of speech readily resorted to song; or so it seemed to Trazel, for in more than one place he observed some who had pushed back tables and chairs and begun impromptu chorales.

When Trazel had his fill of observing the festivities, his mind returned to the prospect before him: a mission to the Circle of Becoming. And the more he thought about it, the more excited he became until, in a frenzy of anticipation, he began to skip wildly about, and actually performed a few cartwheels, much to the amusement of passers-by.

Karam-Bor was left quite embarrassed by these antics, and did his best to act as if he didn't know the young gadabout. But Trazel foiled these efforts by suddenly dashing toward him. In a burst of enthusiasm, he grabbed him by the folds of his robe and whisked him completely around.

"Now see here!" exclaimed Karam-Bor, smoothing his garments and doing his best to salvage his dignity.

"Oh, it's going to be something very important, Karam-Bor," Trazel sang out in an extempore melody. "Oh, very, very important! I can feel it deep inside me!"

"*Everything* carried out in this place is important," was the chill lectury reply. "*Everything!* We don't engage in comparisons around here. We leave that to the Fallen Ones."

"I don't mean it's going to be any *better* than any other mission," said Trazel, a bit crestfallen. "Just ... well, important!"

"We'll find out soon enough. But for the time being, I wish

you would start walking down this street with the decorum
which pertains to your office and this place. After all, you're
not some imp darting about the corridors of the Everlasting
Darkness! And it certainly won't do to go dancing into the
Armaments Office acting as if you didn't know the meaning
of the word responsibility!"

These words caused a delayed reaction. Trazel walked
ahead a few paces before stopping abruptly.

"Armaments — ?" he repeated softly, as if he couldn't
quite believe what he'd heard. "Did you say ... Armaments
Office?"

"I'm afraid I did."

"Does that mean I'm going to be ... armed?"

"That, I regret to say, is what I have been informed."

The news sent Trazel into a delirium of skipping and
hooraying. But then all at once he ceased and turned as
sedate as a headstone.

"You know, Karam-Bor," he confided, "I knew all along
that I'd be given a task so dangerous, so full of treachery and
peril and woe, that I'd need to be armed!"

"That I would describe as a presumption of the first magnitude."

"No, it's quite so! I'm sure of it. And I'll tell you something
else too. I think I already know what they're going to give
me!"

"And, pray, what do you suppose that might be?"

"They're going to give me ... " said Trazel, pausing a moment for dramatic effect, *"thunderbolts!"*

"Thunderbolts?" exclaimed Karam-Bor with a decorous
laugh.

"Oh, don't laugh, Karam-Bor! I know deep inside me it's
going to be thunderbolts!"

"Well, I certainly hope not! Because if you want my
opinion, Trazel, you're far too frisky to be entrusted with

thunderbolts."

"No, Karam-Bor, I disagree entirely. You only know one side of me. The truth is that I can be as serious as anyone when I have to be. If they gave me thunderbolts, I assure you I'd be very careful. And besides, I've been told I have an awfully good aim."

"Everyone your age says he has a good aim," observed Karam-Bor. "When I was at your stage of things, I felt quite convinced that no one in the Kingdom had quite so good an aim as yours truly."

"Well," said Trazel with a sigh. "Maybe you did. And maybe you didn't. I'll leave comparisons to the Fallen Ones. All I can tell you is that there's been more than one that's told me I have an excellent aim."

"Then you should know you need *more* than an excellent aim. You need an *expert* aim! I mean, those thunderbolts can be very tricky. They don't always go where you want them to. You need a keen sense of anticipation or you'll do immense damage. ... And if you wonder how I happen to know all this," Karam-Bor added by way of clinching the argument, "it's because I myself was once considered for thunderbolts."

The younger responded with an admiring look.

"You *were?*"

"Indeed I was. My mentor said quite distinctly, 'Let Karam have thunderbolts.'"

"And did you get them?"

"As a matter of fact, I did not. ... Not that I couldn't *handle* them, mind. It's just that there were other things to be done."

"So what did they give you?"

"Well, the first time, as I recall, they gave me the power of disappointment."

"The power of *disappointment?* Oh, what a disappointment!"

"Disappointment, nothing! It takes great subtlety to wield

the power of disappointment."

"Still you must have been disappointed."

"I was *not*! I knew as well as anyone that disappointment has no place in our order of things. That's why I contented myself to do the very best job I could with the weapon chosen for me."

The two walked on for a considerable distance before the conversation became rekindled. Trazel spoke.

"Karam-Bor, I've been meaning to ask you for a long time how many missions you've been given."

"Just two."

"Someone told me that this was the reason you had two names."

"Indeed so. You yourself will be given a second name after your second mission. But you won't get a third until after the twelfth. And the fourth must wait until the twenty-second."

"And will you have as many as twenty-two missions?"

"It's a question I do not ask. I'm here to serve, not speculate."

"But what would happen if there were no more missions for you?"

"I think I should cease to exist. That's all."

"But that would be *terrible!*"

"Not if the sole reason for your existence were service," said Karam-Bor dryly.

They had now reached the far limits of the Great Hall. The end of it proved to be a temporary barrier made of fencing and huge sheets of canvass. From the other side came sounds of construction.

"Still at it!" Karam-Bor muttered to himself. "Busy, busy, busy — "

"Do you think the Great Hall will ever be finished?" Trazel asked.

"Not," stated Karam-Bor, "if He insists on inviting more

guests than He has room for. The way it strikes me, sometimes, this thing could go on getting bigger and bigger forever!"

"Would that be bad?"

"I've never given it much thought, to tell you the truth."

Trazel did think about it awhile. But then a new line of in-
quiry came to him.

"Karam-Bor, will you and I ever get a chance to go to the
Banquet ourselves?"

"Alas, no."

"Why?"

"It's strictly invitation-only."

"Then how do you finagle an invitation?"

"You don't *finagle* and invitation! It ... it's simply offered."

"You must be very smart or good to get one — "

"Hah! That's a laugh! You should see some of the riff-raff
who've been asked to come! No, Trazel, He's generous to a
fault in that respect. Just tosses out invitations left and right.
But at the same time he won't issue an invitation unless it can
be as easily refused as accepted. Unless you can say No as
easily as Yes, depend upon it, there's no invitation for you!"

"Why is that?"

"I suppose it's because He only wants friends here. And to
be a friend, the choice has to be mutual. The problem for you
and me is that our prior knowledge makes it impossible to exercise free choice. We'd say Yes to His invitation all right.
But we'd hardly say No."

"Are you saying there are some who actually refuse?"

"*Refuse*? Why, there are those who tear up the invitation
in His face! They shake their fists at Him, and tell Him to be
gone!"

"Is it possible?" Trazel gasped.

"Oh yes! Indeed it is! In the Circle of Becoming there are

no restraints on one's attitude towards Him."

"But what more could they want than His Banquet, for heavens' sake?"

"A banquet of their own devising, I imagine."

"How drab!"

"For sure! All that junk food! And yourself as guest of honor! It's quite hideous, no doubt about it. But as they say, *de gustibus non disputandem.*"

"What does that mean?"

"There's no accounting for taste."

Trazel contemplated these matters for a time. They seemed to him enormously complicated — rather like six jigsaw puzzles all mixed together.

After awhile he asked: "But why, I wonder, does He put up with it all? Why bother with those who refuse His generosity? I mean, why even bother with those who accept? He doesn't need the one or the other! He doesn't need a Banquet. He doesn't need a Great Hall that's forever unfinished. He doesn't need fireworks or a Circle of Becoming. He doesn't need to go on pushing back the borders of the Everlasting Darkness. Why, He doesn't even need *us!* So why does He bother with it all?"

"Why should I bother with your everlasting questions?" asked Karam-Bor, a bit vexed.

"Because I want to know!"

"Then let me inform you, my dear young friend, that you are dealing with questions for which there are no answers."

"But you must have some idea of what's behind it all!"

"Well, just this. ... I remember something an old-timer with five names once told me when I asked him something of the same. He said that the only reason he could ever come up with for all of these invitations and banqueting and whatnot was that He seems incurably social."

CHAPTER 3
The Sword with the Jasper Handle

The two continued up the avenue. Gradually the park-like surroundings through which they had been strolling changed to a more rural setting. What had begun as a stately, formal boulevard turned by degrees into a country road which led off on a gentle ramble through grain fields and pastures and vineyards.

As they walked along, Karam-Bor began to describe to Trazel something of the geography of the region. The youngster listened with all proper respect, not failing to ask the sorts of questions which the elder could answer with an impressive display of erudition.

Trazel found himself especially intrigued by the great sea, which the road approached and bordered for a while. From the shore the two could see clearly the fantastic creatures suspended in its crystal waters, as well as the exotic colors and contours of the sea bottom.

From there the road led upward into the bracing air of snow-covered mountains. At the summit of one of the tallest, they turned around to see where their way had taken them so far. There below lay the great sea, and beyond the gently rolling patchwork of the countryside. Still farther off could be seen the Great Hall with its new construction on the near side, and the battlements of the Kingdom on the far — all of it a brilliant contrast to the swirling mists of light in the Circle of Becoming and the Everlasting Darkness beyond.

On the other side of the mountain they could make out a path which would take them down through a splendid forest of evergreen and on into a valley which cradled a broad, majestic river. A bridge spanned the river, and from there a road began a gradual ascent up the far slope of the valley until it reached a promontory on which could be seen the dazzlingly white dome of an imperious building surrounded by twelve smaller structures of a similar architecture.

"What is it?" Trazel inquired in awe.

"Operations," murmured Karam-Bor, as though nothing could be more ordinary.

"Is that where we find out about our mission?"

"It is."

"And where I'll get my thunderbolts?"

"If thunderbolts it's going to be — "

"Then let's *hurry*, Karam-Bor! Let's *run* before they change their minds!"

"Changing minds is not exactly standard operating procedure around here," Karam-Bor responded a trifle stiffly.

"Still it wouldn't hurt to get there as fast as we can."

"If getting there as fast as we can is an exercise in impatience, then it *would* hurt. No, I say let us carry on as before."

Trazel appeared downcast by these instructions. Nevertheless, he set off at a greatly accelerated pace, stopping only to turn around every so often to cast an imploring look at Karam-Bor behind him.

When they reached the edge of the plaza on which the buildings stood Karam-Bor took hold of Trazel's robe and pulled him to a stop.

"Now Trazel, listen to me," he said. "I would very much prefer for the two of us to *walk*, not run, from here to the entrance of Operations Central. What is more, I would like to walk in such a way that I do not find myself a spectacle of major proportions. So I'm going to ask of you a favor. The merest ... trifle."

"What would that be, Karam-Bor?"

"Simply that from here to there you propel yourself forward at a pace which shall not exceed my own. Do you understand?"

"Of course, Karam-Bor! I wouldn't think of getting there any other way!"

"That," said Karam-Bor, "has not been my experience, I'm sorry to say. And it is that same experience, I might add, which prompts me to offer an incentive. So pay heed! *If,* my eager young friend, *if* you do me the courtesy of matching your pace with mine, not permitting yourself to advance so much as a half-stride ahead of my own, I will repay you with a favor of your own at some future date."

"Oh, you don't need to do *that,* Karam-Bor!"

"Ah, but I insist! The carrot rather than the stick, don't you see? A reward! Why, we do all sorts of things for rewards, don't we? So just remember to walk ever so calmly and ever so deliberately right here beside me. And some day you'll have a favor all your own. Agreed?"

"Absolutely! Upon my honor!"

And Trazel was as good as his word. He walked inconspicuously at Karam-Bor's side across the not inconsiderable expanse of the great plaza all the way to the magnificent rise of marble steps which led to the entrance of the main building.

But when Trazel saw a sign of brushed platinum set in stone on which OPERATIONS CENTRAL had been engraved in large letters, and below a long list of departments, bureaus and sections, with the words "Armaments Office" somewhere toward the bottom, he threw all restraint to the winds and took the steps three at a time all the way to the top. And when he arrived there breathless, he turned around and gestured wildly for Karam-Bor to follow suit.

Karam-Bor paid no attention whatever, but mounted the stairs at his usual stately pace.

"I'm afraid," he remonstrated quietly when he reached Trazel, "that you broke your end of the bargain."

"But you didn't say anything about *steps*, Karam-Bor," was the guileless reply. "You only told me to walk slowly across the *plaza*."

"Perhaps we need a written contract. One with all the i's dotted and the t's crossed. Is that what you're saying?"

"No, but — "

"But from now on our agreement covers the entire area! *All* of it! The plaza. The stairs. The hallways and rooms and nooks and crannies, and any other place, location or zone which is here, or will be here, or may be imagined to be here! Is that quite understood?"

"Certainly, Karam-Bor! Certainly!"

"Certainly indeed! Well, all right. We start from the beginning once more, thus: if you keep yourself from dashing about like some fireworks gone berserk, then you'll have your favor."

"When?"

"Whenever you ask. And believe me, if I can be spared your bubbling and frothing for just a little while, just long enough until we're safely out of here, I'll be only too glad to give you your favor."

With that the two entered Operations Central.

Trazel noticed that the floor inside the building was constructed of a crystal-like substance which distributed light so perfectly that there wasn't a shadow to be seen anywhere.

Clusters of beings like themselves could be seen engaged in various activities. Karam-Bor seemed to know most of them, for he nodded greetings to this one and that as he and Trazel proceeded on into the vestibule and down the main corridor.

It took quite a while before the two arrived at last at a

minor passageway near the rear of the building with a sign at its head which read "Armaments Office." An arrow pointed off to the right.

A bit farther along the two passed through a set of double doors into a large, warehouse-looking affair dominated by a long counter. The room lay quite deserted, save for an elderly sage in a far corner who was passing his time plucking a stringed instrument and humming a melody. So lost was he in his music that he failed to notice the advent of Trazel and Karam-Bor.

"Ahem!" said Karam-Bor.

The being looked up, startled.

"Oh! Ah! A customer at last!" he cried.

Laying down his instrument, he approached the counter with the air of one determined to please. He smiled at the two of them, then gave Karam-Bor a second glance.

"Why if it isn't Karam-Bor," he exclaimed. "My, my, my! Haven't seen you in ages!"

"Three of them, to be exact. And I must say I'm surprised to find you still here, Valkor-Maar-Qen."

"Yes, still here. Keeping out of mischief. ... And it would seem you do the same. I gather you were successful with your last mission."

"Quite successful, thank you. But it wasn't any picnic, I can tell you that! The Fallen Ones were everywhere, stirring up trouble. We had some close calls, I won't deny it. But we managed somehow."

"I congratulate you."

"Not necessary, of course."

"Oh, I know that. But I do so anyway."

The one in charge of armaments now turned and scrutinized the countenance of Trazel.

"And who is your delightful companion?"

"His name is Trazel, He's ... *new*," said Karam-Bor, with

an intonation which as much as said that Trazel could there-
fore be expected to behave oddly. "Trazel, meet Valkor-
Maar-Qen."

"Honored to meet somebody with three names," said
Trazel politely.

"And I am more than honored to meet you, I'm sure," replied Valkor-Maar-Qen. He paused, as though consulting his
memory, and then said, "Seems to me I came across a name
like yours lately. Said yours was Trazel, didn't you?"

"That's it."

"Well, I think there's a requisition here with the name
Trazel on it. Let's see — "

Valkor-Maar-Qen began shuffling through a pile of papers
which lay on the counter.

"Seems to me it was a sword — " he mumbled half-aloud.

"Only a *sword?*" said Trazel, hardly able to quench his disappointment.

Valkor-Maar-Qen then found what he'd been looking for.
He held up the sheet of paper for closer scrutiny.

"One sword, Model Daleth-Delta-Fourteen. Assignee,
Trazel, sixteenth millenial Rank, four hundred sixty-first
Circle, ninth Cohort."

"That's me, all right," said Trazel sadly. "Only I must confess I was hoping for thunderbolts."

"Now, now," said Valkor-Maar-Qen. "Don't fret. They all
hope for thunderbolts, my dear young friend. ... Why, I can
even remember that Karam-Bor here was hoping for thunderbolts on his first assignment. And then he found out that
all he was given — "

"There's no need to go into all that again," Karam-Bor interrupted. "Just give this youngster his sword so we can get
over to our Sector. They're waiting for us."

"But of course, Karam-Bor. How bothersome of me to
keep you waiting. It ... it's just that I like a little conversation

now and then. Things are terribly slow in armaments these days."

"As it should be," said Karam-Bor a bit primly.

"Oh, I agree! This business of force is no good. But then, there are times when even He must do battle. Anyway, I do want your young colleague here to know that the sword he's getting is no ordinary sword."

"But a sword is a sword," said Trazel. "While thunder-bolts — !"

"Ah, but this is a special model. I mean it's quite extraordinary!"

"How so?"

"Well, to begin with, it has a perfectly splendid jasper handle."

"Only jasper?"

"Yes, but the hilt is of platinum! Pure platinum! Cold-forged and annealed to a mirror finish. As for the blade — well, there are blades and blades. But this one descends to an edge of such keenness that it becomes resolved into a fine fire all up and down its entire length, which means you can whirl it about in such a way that it will frighten the wits out of any mortal in the Circle of Becoming."

"Still, it isn't thunderbolts," said Trazel.

"Perhaps if he could *see* the sword," Karam-Bor prompted.

"See? Oh my yes, *see*! An excellent idea, Karam-Bor. Should have thought of it myself, because I'm sure that once this young fellow *sees* the sword, he'll be *glad* he didn't get thunderbolts!"

Valkor-Maar-Qen moved off into a storage room farther back. A few moments later he'd returned bearing the sword with the jasper handle. With it he brought an unusually lavish scabbard encrusted with so many diamonds and emeralds and rubies that the metal which held them could scarcely be seen.

"Actually," Valkor-Maar-Qen explained, with a con-
spiratorial glance at Karam-Bor, "this scabbard doesn't go
with Model Daleth-Delta-Fourteen. But just between the
three of us, I must confess that the regulation scabbard
seemed a little drab to me. Nothing but emeralds and
aquamarines, don't you know. And since this one has been
lying around back there doing nothing, I thought you might
as well use it instead."

Already the sword itself had proved a pleasant surprise for
Trazel, even its handle, which was of a deep, transluscent
green. But the scabbard was more impressive still. The
thought of striding about with such a sword and scabbard
clasped to his side filled Trazel with great excitement. All lin-
gering disappointment now melted away.

"Just sign here in triplicate," said Valkor-Maar-Qen.

Trazel scribbled his name on the three forms, then bound
the scabbard to his robe. The sword with the jasper handle
fitted the scabbard almost perfectly, save for a sliver of space
near the hilt, which leaked tiny spurts of flame.

Trazel presently made a smart military about-face and was
halfway out the door before Karam-Bor called him back with
the suggestion that he thank Valkor-Maar-Qen for his help-
fulness.

Karam-Bor had hoped the combination of the sword and
the agreement might tame some of Trazel's high spirits. But,
if anything, the situation grew more intolerable still. For, al-
though Trazel walked close to Karam-Bor's side, he now
took to swaggering in a way which once more caused no end
of amusement for those nearby. Karam-Bor could only set
his face like stone as they moved across the plaza toward the
building where they would be given their assignment.

CHAPTER 4
The Seventh Sector

It occurred to Karam-Bor, after awhile, that an explanation of the Operations complex might serve to take Trazel's mind from his sword. And so the elder began to tell the younger all about the magnificent building which dominated the center of things here, and the twelve which formed a circle about it.

He told of the over-all Master Plan which determined the configurations of the Circle of Becoming. He told of planning and strategy and deployment throughout the Circle, all coordinated in Operations Central, which had a direct communication link with Him who sat at the Head Table. He told of policy decisions which directly affected all aspects of the Circle of Becoming, from the outskirts of the Kingdom to the very borders of the Everlasting Darkness.

But there was a secondary level of operations too, he pointed out. The Circle of Becoming had been divided into twelve sectors, each under the surveillance of a special staff.

"That's why there are twelve buildings all around the headquarters," explained Karam-Bor. "Each of them has a twelfth of the whole to look out for. Each has a piece of the pie, as it were."

"Can I ask a question?" Trazel inquired politely.

"By all means!"

"Could you please tell me why everything around here is in *twelves?*"

Karam-Bor stopped dead in his tracks. The question had never occurred to him.

"And why shouldn't it be in twelves?" he said rather sharply.

"Oh, I don't know. It's just that I think things would be, well, maybe a bit neater if they were in, say, tens."

"Do you really think so?" said Karam-Bor, a slight distance having crept into his voice. "Then perhaps we could arrange to do everything over to suit you."

"At least it would be faster," offered Trazel.

"Ah, faster. Yes. But then, speed isn't everything, is it?"

"How about ease?"

"Nor is ease everything, I'm afraid."

"Practicality?"

"Practicality isn't everything either."

"Then what *is* everything?"

"*He* is everything. And it so happens that *He* is partial to twelve. Don't ask me why, because I can't tell you. All I can say is that He prefers doing things by the dozen. It's the sort of thing you take or leave, whatever your affinity for tens."

"It was just a thought," said Trazel wistfully.

"Hmmmmph!" said Karam-Bor.

"Understand I'm not complaining."

"I should hope not."

"I'm not carping."

"To your credit, I'm sure."

"So why don't we forget about all that, and let me ask you something else."

"Which is?"

"What sector are we bound for?"

"The seventh."

"And the building we're headed toward, is that where they have charge of the Seventh Sector?"

"For once you are correct."

Trazel felt a renewed surge of anticipation.

"Don't you think we ought to hurry a little, Karam-Bor?"

he now asked.

"Hurry?" repeated Karam-Bor, as though the very thought had been hurled from the depths of the Everlasting Darkness.

"I mean, don't you suppose they're waiting for us?"

"I think we can safely assume that they have a little more to do than wait for us."

Trazel did not argue the point. But he did attempt to speed the pace a little.

"May I remind you of our agreement, Trazel!"

"I do remember. It's my *feet* that keep forgetting!"

"Then remind them of that moment in the future when you say, 'Karam-Bor, it's time for you to do me a favor!' And as I grant that favor gladly, your feet will rejoice along with the rest of you!"

Trazel responded with a sigh. The building ahead seemed to him as far away as ever.

After a time, Trazel's hand found the sword at his side. His fingers touched the polished jasper, then began to weave through the gems which bejeweled the scabbard. It occurred to him that he ought to practice drawing the sword. After all, he reasoned with himself, suppose a Fallen One were to creep up unexpectedly from behind.

And so, with a ringing sound, out flashed the sword. Trazel flourished it about his head, then stabbed and slashed at an imaginary opponent before returning the sword to its scabbard.

This exercise, he discovered, provided him with a great deal of satisfaction. So he repeated it.

"*Now* what are you doing?" Karam-Bor asked wearily.

"Just practicing."

"Practicing what?"

"Practicing getting my sword out of the scabbard. One has to be quick about it sometimes, you know!"

"Well, in case you weren't aware of it, you're making a

spectacle of yourself once more. And I regret to say that since I'm walking beside you, I share in that spectacle."

Trazel looked around, and sure enough, he caught a few amused glances.

"I didn't mean to," he said contritely.

"No doubt. But please! Do me the goodness of saving your energy for a more appropriate time and place."

Trazel gave yet another sigh. It was as though he were the chief of those patient martyrs from the Circle of Becoming of whose lives Karam-Bor was wont to read aloud.

But after awhile Trazel brightened. He said: "They'll be surprised when they see my sword."

"*Who* will be surprised when they see your sword?"

"Those in the building where we're bound."

"I hope this won't come as a great disappointment, but let me assure you that they've seen swords before."

"But none so grand!"

"None so *grand?* On the contrary. They've seen *many* quite as grand. And not a few far *more* grand. And while I'm on the subject, my young chevalier, let me remind you once more that we don't deal in comparisons around here!"

Again Trazel sighed and subsided.

After what seemed to him an eternity, they at last reached their destination. As they stood before the buildin's impressive facade, they could see chiseled onto its great lintel, which which was supported by twelve huge pillars, the words THE SEVENTH SECTOR.

On they proceeded into the vestibule. This in turn opened directly onto a gallery which made a vast circle about the main level below. From this vantage point they looked down on a transparent plot board which stretched the entire length and breadth of the building.

Attendants numbering in the tens of thousands, all of them attired in pale yellow uniforms, quietly went about the business of charting the movements of swirl-shaped clusters of light which were being projected onto the plot board.

Circling the area were stacks of instruments — a myriad of graphs and scanners and digital displays, as well as rows upon rows of pilot lights, some of which glowed steadily in a veritable rainbow of hues, while others blinked off and on in a random sequence.

Trazel gaped at the sight which opened before him, though Karam-Bor at his side maintained an I've-seen-it-all-before air.

"Now, my dear young colleague," said Karam-Bor a bit pompously, "in case you've been wondering what happened to all those fireworks — "

He stretched out his hand and let the scene below serve as the completion of his sentence.

"Imagine!"

"And that's only a *twelfth* of it. If you went into any of the other eleven buildings you'd see much of the same. So don't suppose those fireworks you were cheering about are just an occasional entertainment. Oh, they make a lot of noise, I know. And they look pretty for awhile. But after that it's work, work, work!"

"And this is how they're followed"?

"Not just followed, my friend. They are followed *meticulously*. They're weighed, measured, analyzed, graphed, charted and subjected to an ongoing program of statistical probability. As you can tell, there are twelve separate clusters of light fragments being watched in this sector alone. That is the most permitted at any one time. What you see below is the main plot board. Here they're observed as they develop in relationship to one another, as well as their positions relative to the Kingdom of Light and the Everlasting Darkness. Then, in twelve separate operation zones around the rear of this building, each is given its own detailed attention."

"I remember asking you once whatever became of His fireworks."

"Well, now you can see for yourself!"

"Yes, I can."

"Note how the light begins to break up as it floats off toward the Everlasting Darkness. The further it moves away from Him, the more shadowy it becomes until, at last, nothing remains but a glimmer at the very borders of the Circle of Becoming. It is then that some are dispatched to go and gather up the fragments. Rescue Squads, they're called. All made up of hand-picked veterans like Valkor-Maar-Qen. And believe me, my young sprite, when I say it's risky work! It's the most dangerous assignment of all!"

"Have you ever gone on such a mission, Karam-Bor?"

"Not yet. I ... I'll need at least three names for that. But the time will come, I suspect. And I shall go. Of course I'd go! And *hope* to get back!"

To Trazel, Karam-Bor at that moment looked about as resolute as it was possible for a being to look. That's when he began to wonder what it would be if he himself were sent out on such a mission, and once more his hand stole toward the sword with the jasper handle. Nothing, he felt, would be too dangerous for him so long as such a sword were clasped to his side.

Meanwhile, those below carried out their work with quiet efficiency.

Suddenly Trazel's reverie was interrupted by a pleasant-sounding buzzer. At the same time, a green circle began to flash off and on near the center of the swirls.

Trazel noticed that there were a number of other pulsing green circles at various points on the plot board, as well as a great many more which burned steadily green. He asked Karam-Bor about them.

"The regular green circles are called Spheres of Operative

Choice. Each indicates a place in the Circle of Becoming where there have come to be creatures capable of making decisions about themselves. In other words, would-be banqueters. A flashing green circle, on the other hand, indicates potential. These are places where exist all of the necessary conditions for Beings of Choice to emerge. Some of our own are likely on the scene now, checking things out."

A different, more strident buzzer also began to sound. Alongside the pulsing green circles, a crimson dagger began to blink.

"And what is that?"

"It indicates the presence of Fallen Ones. Invariably when a Sphere of Operative Choice is about to be established, the Fallen Ones show up."

"And what do they do?"

"Oh, they harry our investigators. Or they try to persuade those who have been given the power of choice that there is no need to accept an invitation to the Banquet."

"No need to come to the *Banquet*? How stupid! Why should they want to do that?"

"Because they would have others be as themselves. It is, you might say, a point of pride."

"If I were a Being of Choice, I would never listen to a Fallen One, I can tell you that, Karam-Bor!"

"It's easy to say as much when you're safe here. But when you find yourself between here and the Everlasting Darkness it's not so simple. I *know,* Trazel. I've *been* there! I've met Fallen Ones who are far more fetching, more persuasive than any of us! There was one in particular who very nearly had me convinced that darkness was light, and light darkness. He told me in the most genteel, cultured language that He who sits at the Head Table is a fraud, and that I — me, Karam-Bor, a two-mission messenger boy — was everything! And I very nearly *believed* him! I shudder when I think of it!"

Now came the ringing of a bell. One of the green circles at
the far rim of the swirl had turned an amber color and begun
to dim.

Attendants crowded round. Some moved toward one of
the instrument boards. Pilot lights were blinking erratically.
Numbers on digital readouts spun in a dizzying sequence.
Then the circle disappeared altogether.

"What was that all about?" Trazel asked.

"I'm afraid one of the Spheres of Operative Choice has
ceased to be."

"What happened?"

"I can't be sure. Perhaps there was a collision of some sort
out there. Perhaps the forces which sustained choice became
unbalanced. Sometimes the Beings of Choice themselves
figure out a way of ending their existence, if you can believe
it! I just don't know about this particular one. All I can tell
you is that they've got what we call an EOA."

"EOA?"

"End of an age."

"But how could something just *end* like that, what with all
this charting equipment and whatnot?"

"That's the point. They *chart* here. Nothing more. Beyond
the parapets of the Kingdom you find that sole condition
which secures the power of choice. It's called freedom. A
great good, freedom. But it has certain limitations too! Because where there is freedom, there is ... chance. And where
there is chance, there are ... well, let us say there are tears."

"But why doesn't He exercise His *power* out there, to keep
these collisions or whatever from happening?"

"Really, it's a most complex problem, and there isn't time
to deal with it now, Trazel. Be content for the moment to
know that He does not interfere with freedom. He has the
power to limit His power, and He does just that. It's the only
way He can confer freedom, with all its wonder and risk. As I

said, freedom sometimes means tears. But it can bring laughter too. It makes it possible to say No to His invitation. But if you can say No, you can say Yes too, can't you? That's why Beings of Choice have the opportunity to become His friends, and come as invited guests to His party. ... But enough of this chit-chat. We have an appointment to keep."

CHAPTER 5
Light Cluster
Kay-Sar-Beta-Null-Two-Common

Twelve domed structures lay in a semi-circle around the rear of the Sector Seven building. Each was connected to the others by walkways of so pellucid a substance that they could scarcely be seen. These soared high over formal gardens in which lawn and boxwood, flower bed and reflecting pool were laid out in a series of intricate labyrinths.

Karam-Bor and Trazel proceeded toward the eleventh of the domes. Once inside they found themselves in an amphitheatre, the floor of which also served as a plot board, though the display was considerably smaller than that of the major building and consisted of but a single swirl of light.

Attendants here wore uniforms of pastel blue. So intent were they at charting the internal movements of the various light particles on the display that no one took notice of the arrival of Karam-Bor and Trazel.

The two remained on the top row of the amphitheatre awhile, observing the doings below. Little by little their fascination, like a magnet, drew them downward, closer and closer to the plotboard, until at last they were standing at its very edge.

It was then that their presence became noticed, for one of the blue-clad workers approached them. He appeared to serve in a supervisory capacity of some sort, for he carried a pointer in one hand and a notebook in the other. Still there was nothing authoritarian in his manner or appearance. Indeed the contrary, for his considerable girth and his broad, open countenance radiated geniality.

"Am I addressing Karam-Bor and Trazel, the novice?" he inquired.

"No one else!" declared Trazel, turning slightly so that the splendor of his scabbard would not be overlooked.

"It should be evident," murmured Karam-Bor, "which is which."

"Ah, but of course! You must be Karam-Bor. And this eager young thing is Trazel. So welcome, Karam-Bor! Welcome, Trazel! My name is Sandor-Xo. I'm the one who's going to explain your mission."

"I thought as much," said Trazel, adding by way of explanation, "your pointer."

"My pointer?"

"It goes with explanations."

"Oh, yes! I see what you mean. Pointing. Explaining. And I'm always at it, it seems."

"Then," said Trazel, edging closer, and adopting an air of confidentiality, "there's something you ought to know at the very outset."

"Something I ought to know?"

"Amen."

"And what could that be?"

"Simply this. Those others. The ones you've pointed things out to before. No matter how ... well, let us say, no matter how apprehensive, even terrified they might have become when you ... you explained what lay ahead, I want you to know that Karam-Bor here and I aren't the least bit nervous!"

At this, Karam-Bor rolled his eyes and heaved a great sigh of despair.

"No matter how dangerous our mission might be," Trazel insisted, "Karam-Bor and I are more than up to it!"

"*Please,* Trazel!" Karam-Bor pleaded.

Sandor-Xo merely smiled.

"Well-spoken," he said. "Pluck is much to be admired! And you're right about the danger part. There are many hazards ahead. But that means you're off on an adventure, too! And adventures are much to be sought after, don't you think?"

Trazel nodded sagely.

"And it will give you the opportunity to put that magnificent sword to work!"

"It *is* a rather extraordinary sword, if I say so myself," said Trazel, patting the handle familiarly.

"Indeed it is! Why, I don't ever remember *seeing* such a splendid sword as that around here!"

Trazel threw Karam-Bor and I-told-you-so look before replying: "And I won't hesitate to use it, I can assure you of that!"

"Could I ask you to draw it for me?" Sandor-Xo inquired.

"Only too glad to. Just be careful you don't touch it."

"Oh yes?"

"I don't want you to hurt yourself."

"Most thoughtful of you, I'm sure."

"You see, it's drawn to such a fine edge that it actually turns to flame."

"Ah, yes! But of course, that's how it is with all our better swords. The idea is to cut through the darkness, don't you know."

"Cut through the darkness?"

Trazel mused over this explanation a few moments, then admitted, "You know, I never thought of that before!"

He considered the matter a while longer, then declared, "Why, I could slice the Everlasting Darkness into little pieces if someone turned me loose."

"A bold idea! Quite audacious, in fact! But ... it would take some doing, I'm afraid. It ... it's quite extensive, you know — the Everlasting Darkness. Still, I can't help admiring your

get-up-and-go. It's the sort of thing you need when you enter
the Circle of Becoming."

"And exactly where in the Circle will we be headed?" asked
Karam-Bor, who had long since tired of the foregoing conversation.

"Well, just walk out here onto the plot board, and I can
give you a quick run-through of your itinerary. After that
we'll wander back to the observatory so you can have an actual look at the places you'll be visiting."

The surface on which they began to walk had the appearance of huge blocks of aquamarine fitted together so that
each formed a latitudinal and longitudinal square. The floor
was perfectly transparent, though of a slightly bluish cast.
The light swirl had been projected in such a way that the display seemed suspended three-dimensionally.

Sandor-Xo offered a brief background on the various
charting procedures, concluding with the information that his
primary responsibility lay with the illuminated green circles
located in various parts of the display.

"As you probably already know, these are what we call
PSOCs. The letters stand for 'Potential Spheres of Operative
Choice.' What that means is that somewhere within these
circles there exist living beings — creatures who emerged
from the dust and debris of the original explosion with lives
all their own. Now they have almost reached the point where
they are capable of that which pertains to Him alone who sits
at the Head Table."

"And what would that be?" Trazel asked.

"The ability to *choose.* To make up their minds. To turn
this way or that. ... You see, it requires an incredibly delicate
balance of all sorts of factors for the power of choice to come
to be. It happens rarely. But when it does, He becomes ever
so interested. For here is the raw material, as it were, for new
friendships."

Sandor-Xo directed his pointer toward three pulsing green circles.

"Now, as you can see, there are only three such areas in this particular light cluster. The two, here and here, are located fairly close to the center of things. The other is off somewhat by itself."

"It does look a little lonely out there," Trazel said.

"A not overly-promising corner of the cluster, I would agree. But then, when I explain the mission you will see that it really doesn't matter *where* a Potential Sphere of Operative Choice is located. What counts are its size, its composition, its density, and its temperature, all as they relate to the three forces which bind everything together."

"No doubt," said Trazel thoughtfully.

Sandor-Xo turned to Karam-Bor.

"Have you told him anything at all about the mission?"

"Alas, no," said Karam-Bor. He lowered his voice a notch, adding: "I regret to say so, but our young friend is not what you would call the listening sort. A bit on the ... oh, I'd say the hyper-active side, if you catch my meaning."

"Of course," said Sandor-Xo, "it might be nothing more serious than an excess of enthusiasm."

He turned to Trazel.

"Actually, your mission is really quite simple. What you and Karam-Bor must do is go out and reconnoiter these three Potential Spheres of Operative Choice. In each of them you will find certain PBOCs, or Potential Beings of Choice. Your duty is to investigate these creatures. Assess their qualities. Judge their capacities. Evaluate their ability to choose wisely and well. Determine if they have in them the potential for friendship with Him who sits at the Head Table. In short, examine these various candidates to see which of the three would provide the most suitable guests for the Banquet. And when you've finished your investigation, you and Karam-Bor must choose the PBOCs on whom you will confer the power of choice. When you have done so, communicate the information to us and we will re-designate the area as a Sphere of Operative Choice, and the creature as a Being of Choice."

"Do you mean that we do the choosing ourselves?"

"Oh yes! You see, that's the beauty of these missions. Your *exercise* of choice becomes the occasion of their *gift* of choice."

"But why doesn't *He* do the choosing, since He *knows* so much?"

"Simply because He will not impose Himself on the Circle of Becoming. He will do nothing to interfere with that freedom which makes genuine choice possible."

"You mean to say that He has no power out there?"

"Oh my, no! He has power, all right! Complete power! It's just that He chooses to rein that power."

"But if he were to venture into the Circle Himself, then surely He would use his power."

"Not necessarily. In fact, He *does* go out there occasionally, whenever things get dicey. But He does so with all the vulnerability of a Being of Choice. And I don't mind telling you, He's taken His share of nasty knocks. But that topic's not for now. What we need to be concerned about is that you understand the nature of your mission."

"I can't speak for Karam-Bor," said Trazel. "But *I've* got the hang of it!"

"You understand that you begin with an investigation of three different PSOCs and PBOCs — "

"Right."

"That you and Karam-Bor decide which of the three would prove most suitable for an invitation to the Banquet — "

Trazel responded with a nod.

"At which point you proceed to bestow the power of choice."

"That's clear enough. But how do we go about giving this great power?"

"Simply by issuing the invitation."

"That's all there is to it?"

"It's quite enough. The moment they hear the invitation, their minds will begin to take on a new dimension."

"And then what happens?"

"There are certain duties you will undertake. I have here an information packet which I will entrust to Karam-Bor. It contains all the data you will need before you make your choice, and all the instructions you will need afterwards. Let me say only that your major responsibility will be to wait."

"*Wait?* Wait for what?"

"To see how things turn out."

"But that could take a very long time!"

"Not really. Time has a way of getting on out there in the Circle. As you can see for yourself, the light cluster even now approaches the Everlasting Darkness. But come along! Let's go to the observatory where you can get an actual look at the places you'll be visiting."

The observatory was a trapezoidal-shaped chamber mounted on a moveable track along the base of the dome. In its dim, tannish light, Karam-Bor and Trazel found a number of comfortably upholstered chairs on swivels. Presiding over all was a larger chair with arms which curved up slightly to form a console full of knobs, dials, keyboards and switches.

Directly in front of the chair lay a broad, rectangular window of unusually thick glass. Deep within its center floated the same light swirl as that projected onto the plot board.

Sandor-Xo directed Karam-Bor and Trazel to places around the control center. He then seated himself and began twisting dials. The light cluster went dim, then grew brighter. It lost focus briefly, then became even more sharply defined than before.

"All right," said Sandor-Xo. "Here we are looking directly out into the Circle of Becoming. What you see before you began as a mere firework. Now it's become transformed into something quite remarkable, wouldn't you say?"

"It's fantastic!" declared Trazel.

"Not bad," said Karam-Bor. "Though I'll admit I've seen more *interesting* configurations in my time."

"No doubt," said Sandor-Xo. "But this one does have certain intriguing characteristics. For example, note the oblongata shape. Here, we'll turn it sideways so you can see how that lovely smear of light particles mounds about the center."

"What's its name?" Trazel asked.

"This one is called Light Cluster Kay-Sar-Beta-Null-Two-Common."

"I wouldn't call it common at all!" Trazel protested. "It's...stupendous! But tell me, how many bits of light does it contain?"

"Oh, billions. Trillions. I can't recall the exact count. It keeps changing, you know. Some die out. Some fire up. Some keep flickering away until they reach the borders of the Everlasting Darkness."

"And those back in the charting area keep watch over every part of it?"

"Well, yes and no. We ... we pay what you might call a *selective* attention. What I mean is, the desolate parts, those areas which are fiery or frozen beyond redemption, don't get much attention. After all, why should they? What interests us far more are those places capable of bringing forth Beings of Choice."

"There must be many such places!" exclaimed Trazel.

"Well, actually not so many as you might think. The variables are quite exclusive. That's why we have but three possibilities at this moment. Let's have a look at them one by one, and perhaps you will see what I mean."

Sandor-Xo removed a slip of paper from his pocket, unfolded it, and began to read the data aloud as he punched information into a keyboard.

"Radius $\phi\sigma$, polyhedral XT27.19, Third Octant, Vector 14, Interface 2d2. ... "

As other buttons were depressed, gradually the light swirl began to enlarge until it spilled over the edges of the window in a great shower of light flakes flying toward them. At last, one particular point of light had become isolated. The magnification process slowed as this single star became centered in the glass, enlarged to half the window's size.

"This particular light force," said Sandor-Xo, "is called Capal-Resh. It is a fragment of the sixteenth magnitude. Because it became separated early in the firework stage, it has now grown somewhat old. You will note the reddish cast — "

A turn of a dial brought the star yet closer.

"Now please observe carefully the space around Capal-Resh. You will see that it has a number of dark satellites. For the most part, these are mere debris — dead orbs of rock and slag."

Sandor-Xo arose and with his pointer isolated a pair of small spheres which circled Capal-Resh in close proximity to one another.

"Note especially these two. We've given them the name 'Twin Captives.' They're two fairly large spheres, or 'planets,' which circle each other, while at the same time both together orbit the light force. At this point in time and space, the various forces which sustain these dual satellites in their juggling act are perfectly balanced. I'm afraid, though, that their momentum will eventually slow by the merest fraction. When that happens, they will crash into one another and form a larger planet still — one so huge that no form of choice-life will be possible. But right now, on one of the twins you will find creatures capable of receiving the power of choice."

Sandor-Xo brought the Twin Captives into closer range.

"We find it something of an oddity, the way it all came about. In most respects, these spheres are not conducive to choice-life. There is simply too much bulk to them. Potential Beings of Choice require a rather delicate environment. They are so fragile, so wispy that they would ordinarily be crushed by the weight force of planets such as these. But in this case, the spheres are motionless, held rigid by the forces which both attract and repel them. What this means is that on the inner face of each, the gravity is slightly off-set by that of the opposing planet."

Sandor-Xo arose and approached the glass.

"Note this region here," he said, his pointer tapping the glass. "You might almost say that the sphere is wearing a green cap. The color is caused by a dense, green mist. Underneath it lies an area of thick vegetation. It is here that you will find the first of your candidates."

Returning to his chair, Sandor-Xo threw a switch.

The Twin Captives began to recede rapidly. Capal-Resh appeared in a flare of brilliance, then dwindled to a point of light. Quickly, light fragments by the millions recessed until the entire light swirl lay once more serenely suspended in the glass.

Once more Sandor-Xo began to murmur data aloud as he enter it into the focusing mechanism.

"Radius $\beta\omega$, Polyhedral M471.03, 7th Octant, Vector 11, Interface 31Z4 ... "

Again the device telescoped onto a single speck of light floating against the blackness of the Everlasting Darkness.

"If I remember correctly," said Sandor-Xo, "this one is called Olanthros-Tau. You can tell by its whiteness that it is a much newer light force than Capal-Resh. It too has its captives. In this case there are but four, and all of them quite large. In fact, one is so large that at some point it could easily break into flame. It is this planet, Behazi, which accomodates our Second Potential Sphere of Operative Choice. Not the planet itself, mind you. But rather one of the spheroids which circles about it. As we move in closer, you will see that Behazi has eleven satellites all its own. It is the seventh of these that you'll be visiting."

Further magnification, and the spheroid indicated by Sandor-Xo floated before them. It resembled a ball of softest cotton, so thick and white the clouds which surrounded it.

"This moon," explained Sandor-Xo, "is curious in that it has a surface which is sometimes water and sometimes ice. There is a continual process of freezing and thawing on this sphere, depending on whether it is in Behazi's shadow or not. One result is a sea creature who, over a considerable length of time, has grown resourceful enough to turn this process to its own advantage. Without attempting to influence you in any way, let me say that there is something of a consensus here that these creatures would make especially appropriate guests for the Banquet."

Having said as much, Sandor-Xo depressed the cancelling switch.

The Seventh Moon of Behazi began to recede. Light fragments blurred and collapsed inward until once more Light Cluster Kay-Sar-Beta-Null-Two-Common occupied the center of the glass.

New data was programmed into the apparatus.

"This last one is called. ... Let's see. I'm not sure I even remember the name of it. You remember, the one off towards the edge of things — "

As he spoke, a pinpoint of fire became isolated before them and gradually began to enlarge.

"This one, I believe, has nine attendants."

"Look at the one with all the rings!" exclaimed Trazel.

"Yes, that's the most spectacular of the lot. But dead, so far as potential choice-life is concerned. No, it's the third of them that shows certain possibilities. Let me bring it up."

A sphere mottled blue and white sailed into view.

"Note the color," said Sandor-Xo. "It is a mixture of water and cloud and land mass. Somewhere in all of it you will find your third Potential Being of Choice. A rather ungainly sort, I'm given to understand. And not at all agreeable. Anyway, it's all there in the information packet."

A touch of a switch, and the display in the glass vanished.

Lights in the observatory grew brighter.

From the side of his chair, Sandor-Xo picked up an attache case with a chain attached. He swiveled toward Karam-Bor.

"Here is the information packet. In it you will find all the instructions and data you need for your mission."

"I've had experience with this before," said Karam-Bor.

"Then I need say no more."

Sandor-Xo swiveled a bit farther until he directly faced Trazel.

"As for you, Trazel, I am going to deliver the standard speech given all novices. I'm sure that Karam-Bor here has already given you a bushel full of warnings. I hate to repeat them. But still, you're off on a hazardous mission, and you can't be too careful."

"I already know what you're going to say," said Trazel. "You're going to warn me about the Fallen Ones. ... Well, Sandor-Xo, you needn't worry. Not for a moment. Between me and my sword, we're more than a match for any Fallen One!"

"I hope so. Only remember, Trazel, it's easy to feel confident here in the Kingdom. Here His power lies over us like a shield. But when you venture out there where He has chosen to limit His power, it is quite another matter. For that is the realm where the Fallen Ones roam freely. They will find you, make no mistake of it! They will find you and tempt you. Nor will that temptation be at the level of those things you loathe. No, they will make their attack at the level of your highest ideals!"

"Still, my sword — "

"Even your *sword* can be your downfall! For it can tempt you to rely on your own strength. And if you come to that, you yourself shall become as one of the Fallen Ones. And in your pride, you will raise your standard against Him. You will proclaim yourself God, and muster your armies, and suppose that some day you shall invade the very precincts of this place where we now dwell. But your only reward, as you know, shall be eternities of adamantine darkness. That is why I must counsel you, Trazel, with all the seriousness I can muster, to be on your guard!"

"I shall. I promise."

"One hint, Trazel. One little hint. Beware of compliments! They're a sure sign that a Fallen One is somewhere around!"

Trazel nodded sagely. Only now he'd begun to wish that Sandor-Xo would be done with his sermon so that the adventure could begin.

CHAPTER 6
The Twin Captives

Upon entering the Circle of Becoming, the two found themselves overtaken by a sudden chill. Wrapping their robes closely, they sped on toward the blossom of radiance in the Seventh Sector called Light Cluster Kay-Sar-Beta-Null-Two-Common.

When they reached its outer limits, Karam-Bor took bearings. The two then set course for the light force Capal-Resh.

Soon the star loomed before them. Karam-Bor and Trazel looped around it, then took up a position from which they could observe both the star and the double satellites known as the Twin Captives.

These latter spheres, they could see, were whirling about so near each other and at so great a velocity that they were kept in thrall, motionless and facing one another.

On one, the chances of galactic chemistry had ordained an abundance of free water. Over a considerable period of time this water had been drawn, tidal-fashion, to the inner hemisphere, and there a generation of organic life had occurred.

Gradually this life took on a remarkable complexity, occupying a plateau of continental dimensions which lay blanketed in a velvety green mist. From above, the plateau appeared as a smear of verdurous color, and proved of such contrast to the rock and dust hues of the remainder of the planet that even the imperturbable Karam-Bor expressed awe at its beauty.

When the two had descended through the mist to the surface of the plateau, they found themselves in a dense, hot jungle thickly populated with plant life. The appearance of growing things was marked primarily by the force of gravity. For even while the gravitational tug of one planet partially off-set that of the other, the over-all force was such that the vegetation had made all necessary compensations. Trees stood conical like hills. Plants had a flat, collapsed look about them. Vines like great green hawsers intertwined branches and leaves, muscling for a share of the light.

There was no standing water anywhere in the jungle; and yet moisture saturated its thick, spongy soil. Drawn upward by capillary action to the topmost foliage of the jungle flora, the water was there transformed by the light force into the thick, organism-laden mist which covered the plateau. Forming on leaves and branches, the mist would turn to huge droplets, which fell continuously to the floor of the jungle below.

As they strolled along, Karam-Bor and Trazel observed that the vegetation, which at first appeared too crowded to be distinguishable, showed an unusual variety. Some plants were compact and exquisite. Some formed themselves into thick, moss-like blankets. Some had a draped look to them, the result of the pull of gravity. Some showed unusual mobility, snaking smoothly and rapidly among roots and stalks in search of nourishment. There was even a variety of rootless plants — clay-colored predators which congregated in packs at the dusty edges of the uplands, and from there made forays into the jungle in a quest for green food.

Even as Karam-Bor and Trazel watched, a number of such hunters set upon a handsome plant with thick, pod-like leaves and delicate lavender flowers. The predators' heads burrowed into the stem, and consumed its vital fluids. Gradually the plant's color began to fade until nothing remained but a whitish, wilted mass of leaves.

"What sort of creature are we looking for, Karam-Bor?"

Trazel asked.

Karam-Bor drew from the information packet a data sheet with the heading: POTENTIAL BEINGS OF CHOICE/TWIN CAPTIVES.

As he scanned the opening paragraph, he murmured, "It says here they're called Versidians."

"Versidians, eh? And how do we recognize these Versidians?"

"Listen to what it says: 'Versidians are moderately large, ranging seven and eight to the fourteenth power, upsilon wavelength."

"Hmmmmm. That's large enough. ... And are they intelligent?"

"Ayin, on the mem-lamed scale."

"Not bad at all."

"Essentially, the Versidians are plants. According to this description they're herbivorous, mineralivorous and luxivorous."

"Which means?"

"They consume other plants, besides drawing nourishment from the soil and light-sustenance from Capal-Resh."

Karam-Bor continued to peruse the document in silence until a gasp brought him to a stop.

"And what," he said, looking up, "do you suppose is their most distinguishing characteristic?"

"I can't imagine."

"They have two heads."

"*Two* heads? *Two*?

Karam-Bor nodded.

"Oh come on, Karam-Bor! Who are you trying to kid?"

"*Whom* are you trying to kid. And the answer is, no one. Listen: 'During their developmental stage, Versidians evolved two heads, each of which is attached by a long, graceful neck to the central body mass.' "

"It really says that?"

"Do you suppose I'm making this up?"

"I didn't mean that, Karam-Bor. Only that it sounds so strange."

"Then let me go on: 'Each head is equipped with mouth, breathing openings, scent and sound collectors, but only one eye. Nor does this eye *see,* in the conventional sense. It is rather a scanning band which extends nearly halfway around the Versidian's head, being served by a lenticular lens.' "

"Glory! Now that's what I call *weird,* Karam-Bor!"

"Not your every day Potential Being of Choice, I'll admit."

"I mean, if we show up with something like *that* for the Banquet, we'll frighten the lot of 'em! And when I say that, I don't even know what color it is!"

"Versidians are green."

"Green?"

"Actually, dark green."

"Oh! *Dark* green! I suppose that means we should be grateful they're not blue-green or chartreuse or something."

"Well, they *are* plants, aren't they? So what else could you expect a plant to be? Anyway, according to the data sheet, the scales which cover their bodies are rather in the nature of sophisticated leaves. Here's what it says. 'When laid flat, they take on a hard, impregnable character, serving as armor. But they can also be raised to an erect position, and even swiveled somewhat, so as to catch the rays of the light force, upon which the Versidian depends for an important part of its food supply."

"Are they able to move about?"

"Oh yes. ... It says they're among the most mobile of creatures in the Potential Sphere of Operative Choice. They have eight pair of legs along the underbody — "

"Did you say eight?"

"Eight pair."

"That makes *sixteen* altogether?"

"Presumably. But let me finish. 'When they remain in one place for any length of time, these legs sink into the soil like roots in order to draw up nutrients — ' "

And so Karam-Bor continued to read until he'd completed the physical description of the Versidians.

As a result, there was no mistaking the first of these creatures when they came upon it. They found a Versidian sunk deeply into the soil, with one of its heads foraging for food, and the other kept in an upright position, as though a sentinel. As they watched, they became aware of a miniature replica of the creature on the far side. The two of them had found a dim shaft of light from Capal-Resh, and were absorbing its energy into their raised scales even as they went on consuming foliage.

Karam-Bor took out the data sheet and quickly scanned the information relative to the Versidians' eligibility as Potential Beings of Choice.

"We're told," he explained to Trazel, "that these creatures have now come fairly near the mind of Him who is their source. They know joy. They know sorrow. They know fear. They communicate with each other. But what is more important still, they communicate with themselves."

"With *themselves,* you say?"

"Yes. They carry on, so to speak, something of an internal dialogue."

"With two heads, it ought to be fairly easy," said Trazel, sniggering a bit at his own cleverness.

"Your humor," replied Karam-Bor sternly, "will lead you astray, if you're not careful. To be able to carry on a conversation with oneself just happens to be a sure sign of nearness to Him who sits at the head Table."

"So what do they *say* to themselves, Karam-Bor?"

"They say, 'Who are you?' 'What are you doing here?'

'Where are you bound?' That sort of thing."

"And how do they answer such questions?"

"Rather superficially, at this point. ... Ah, but if they were to be invited to the *Banquet!*"

"It would deepen their questions, all right. But really, Karam-Bor, you've got to admit they don't look much like your average banqueter."

"True. But then, most of the creatures you come across in the Circle of Becoming are a little on the peculiar side. You've just got to keep telling yourself that it's the interior part that counts."

"I suppose so."

"And besides, they'll be given new outfits for the Banquet. New bodies. New clothing. New mentalities. As you know, you don't dare enter the Hall unless your get-up, as they say, is impeccable."

"Well, that's a blessing, Karam-Bor. Because these Versidians would look very strange in the Great Hall as they are. And I mean *very!*"

"For what it's worth, my young friend, let me assure you that however strange they look to us, they look quite all right to one another."

As he spoke these words, Karam-Bor found himself overtaken by the eerie sensation that someone was standing directly behind him.

He jumped a bit, turned and, sure enough, found himself face to face with a being rather like himself, only much rounder, much jollier-looking, rather in the tradition of Sandor-Xo.

"Wh- Wh- Who are *you*?" Karam-Bor stuttered, a bit too surprised to be polite.

"Name of Ramey-Do, matter of fact. On my way back from a mission. Saw your trails of light, and thought I'd stop by for a look-see. Sorry if I gave you a fright."

"Well you did, if you must know! For a moment there, I thought a Fallen One was about to pounce on me!"

"A *Fallen* One?" cried Ramey-Do. A cheery laugh rang out. "That's a good one! Tell me now, do I look like a Fallen One?"

"I didn't mean to imply — "

"Oh come on now! Don't be so serious! And don't worry about Fallen Ones either! I don't think there's a single solitary renegade within a million billion miles of here!"

"Well, that's a relief to hear, Ramey-Do. So let me calm myself and make some introductions. I'm Karam-Bor. And this is my colleague, the novice Trazel."

"Pleased to meetcha," said Trazel agreeably.

"And the same to you, I'm sure," replied Ramey-Do. He turned to Karam-Bor. "On assignment?"

"What else would we be doing here?"

"Why ... nothing, now you mention it."

"Actually, we're here to determine if those creatures over there should be given an invitation or not," said Trazel.

"Really? Strange looking beasties, I must say."

"Just what I said myself! But Karam-Bor says there are stranger still to be seen."

"Oh my, I can vouch for that! The Circle is crammed with freaks! And these? Well, they rank right up there with the best!"

"I was wondering," said Trazel, "why one is so much larger than the other."

"That's easy. The larger, you see, gave life to the smaller. It's what they call a mother — something like that. The small creature came right out of her body."

"Ugh!" said Trazel.

"The ideas is for the mother to tend the little one until it gets as big as she."

"Then that's why they stand so close together. But tell me,

Ramey-Do, this business of two heads. Whatever would they want with two of them?"

"I'm not entirely sure. I would guess that one is used primarily for eating, the other for spotting enemies. Mothers especially are concerned that nothing come along to devour their little ones."

"But who would want to *eat* a thing like that?"

"Watch!" said Ramey-Do.

He'd no sooner spoken than a fist-like ball of tendrils came sailing through the air and struck the smaller creature with a grievous blow. Suckers immediately began to writhe among the erect green scales so that they could not be drawn down. At the same time, the creature began to be dragged toward the center of a vine cluster.

The small one, stunned momentarily, at last emitted a piteous cry.

Made suddenly aware of the plight of its child, the mother went into a frenzy, tearing at the tendrils with both of her mouths. Even as she did so, another ball of writhing vines came sailing through the air. This time it struck her. But there was no grappling the larger Versidian, for the leaf-like appendages on her body now lay flat, an emerald-hard plate of armor.

Meanwhile, the smaller was struck again and again by wads of tendrils. Nor was it in the power of the larger to fend them off, or to keep her offspring from being drawn relentlessly into the vortex of the vine cluster.

She now began to emit loud roars of alarm. These summoned others of her kind. Within moments a half score of such creatures had engaged in battle with the vine. The strongest of them gave no heed to the slithering tendrils which entwined the youngster, but instead headed directly for the central mass and began tearing huge chunks of green with its teeth.

It was this attack which tipped the balance. At length the vine disengaged itself, wrapping its thicker parts into a large, impenetrable sphere.

The creatures quickly severed the remaining tendrils which held the young one. But it soon became evident that the infant had been mortally wounded. It lay on its side, its scales in disarray, its heads limp, whimpering occasionally. The mother, assisted by the larger creatures, carressed the body of the youngster. After a time, a gentle effort was made to raise the creature.

But the effort failed. The child gave one final shudder, then lay still.

The attention of the Versidians now focused on the mother. They stood around her in a circle, touching her with their heads and making soft, moaning tones. She seemed too stricken with grief to be aware of their ministration. Nor did she turn to look as a host of worm-like plants emerged from the ground and quickly devoured the body of the young creature.

Trazel, who'd never observed anything like this before, was quite overcome by the sadness of it all. He took to sniffling.

"Of course it isn't fair," Ramey-Do declared with dark indignity. "I don't know why they're obliged to put *up* with such pain."

"True," said Karam-Bor with a sigh.

"The injustice of it all!" declared Ramey-Do.

"I agree," said Karam-Bor. "I tell you, I see something like this and I'm bound to wonder why things are run the way they are. You'd think He'd use His power to prevent such atrocities, wouldn't you?"

"*If* He has such power," murmured Ramey-Do.

The suggestion shocked Karam-Bor at first. But then a philosophical expression crept into his face.

"Well, they do say that He limits His power intentionally."

"True. I've heard that argument before."

"In the interests of freedom, you know."

"An interesting theory, no doubt. But then, of course, it could be ... well, an *excuse,* couldn't it? I mean, *anyone* could say he has power, but just doesn't want to use it."

"A telling point! And well put! I must give it some thought. And just between you and me, Ramey-Do, I keep asking myself why we need this Circle of Becoming at *all!* I mean, this never-ending mayhem and mess! All these creatures and invitations and whatnot! I plain can't understand it! And we *certainly* don't need an Everlasting Darkness! I mean, what's the *point?*"

"Very neatly put! Bravo, Karam-Bor! Really, you have some important things to say!"

"Do I?"

"I should say you do! Too bad there aren't more to hear what I'm hearing!"

"Well, I never thought my ideas were all *that* important! But still, I've had a thought or two in my time, I'll admit that!"

"I'd like to hear more of them!"

"You would?"

"Definitely!"

"Well, sometimes when I have a moment or two to myself, when I'm not being hounded by work or pestered by novices, I find myself wondering if the *real* power might not lie behind that curtain of darkness there."

"You mean with the one they call the Prince of Darkness?" Karam-Bor nodded.

"You think *He* can be the one?"

"I've considered it."

"Well all I can say, Karam-Bor, is that you may be closer to the truth than you think!"

"Truly?"

"Absolutely! All I'd say is that you've got a little displacement problem. Because it's *not* way out there! It's *not* so far away as the Everlasting Darkness! No, my insightful friend! You're searching too far! Too far! Look ... *closer!*"

"Closer?"

"Yes. ... Look — "

"Look *where?*" said Karam-Bor, overtaken by a rush of inexplicable excitement.

"Look ... inward!"

"Inward? You mean the real power is ... is ..."

"Where *else*, Karam-Bor? Where else could it possible *be?*"

"Inside! Inside *me?*"

"But how *wise* you are, Karam-Bor! I ... I'm amazed, really astonished at your *profundity,* your ... *depth!*"

"It's nothing," was the modest reply.

"On the contrary! It's *everything! Everything!* Isn't that so, Trazel?"

"I'm not so sure."

"Oh come on there, young fellow! You've got to admit that your mentor here must be the wisest, the most sagacious, the most clever being to be found anywhere!"

"Well, I've always regarded him as wise. But to go so far as all that — "

"Why, I should think that simple respect for your elders — "

"It's not that, Ramey-Do. What bothers me is something that Sandor-Xo said just as we were about to leave."

"And what did Sandor-Xo say?" said Ramey-Do, suddenly wary.

"He said that if someone came along and started telling us how *smart* we were, it was a sure sign that a Fallen One was somewhere around."

These words, like a clap of thunder, brought Karam-Bor out of the near trance into which he'd fallen. He gave Ramey-

Do a long, searching look.

"Oh m-m-m-m-my!" he stammered.

"Oh my?" responded Ramey-Do with a bemused look.

"You *are* one, aren't you? You *are* a Fallen One! You ... you lied! You told us there wasn't a Fallen One within a million billion miles of us! And all the time you were one yourself! It was a lie! And the rest was lies too! But then, lies are a part of your game, aren't they?"

"What are you saying, my dear friend?"

"Dear friend, nothing! You're no friend of ours! You're no friend of anyone but yourself! Yes, and I wouldn't be surprised if it was you that caused that poor little creature to suffer so! And just to trap us! Just to bring us to a state of rebellion! *Well*? Isn't that *so*?"

Ramey-Do drew himself up. A mask of disdain came over his face.

"You say I lie. But I ask you, what are lies? What? What? I'm sure I don't know. It's all so relative, you know. It's a point of *view*. But in case you should want to hear something that is definitely *not* a lie, then listen to this. ...First of all, I remember you Karam-Bor! Oh, you may not remember me! But I remember you! And what I thought then, I continue to think now. Namely, that the trouble with you, Karam-Bor, is that you're really quite stupid. And not only stupid; you're boring as well. I mean, has anyone ever *told* you that? Told you you're dull? That there's not an once of wit in you? That you're the sort who turns everything into yawns? Hmmmmm? And as for that *dolt* over there — that drab piece of razzle-dazzle named Trazel, that nitwit-nincompoop with the peach fuzz, that — "

Trembling now, Karam-Bor reached into the information packet and drew forth a small card edged in gold. In a high, wavering voice he read:

"Guard us, O source of Light and Power

Grant us strength in danger's hour!"

Ramey-Do began to laugh.

"That stupid incantation has no force out here!" he shouted.

But even as these words rang out, the voice of the Fallen One hollowed. Ever so gradually he disappeared.

Karam-Bor seated himself and let his head fall into his hands.

He began to moan.

In an effort to cheer him, Trazel said, "My, I'm sure glad to see him go!"

"Oooooo," moaned Karam-Bor.

"He seemed quite nice at first!"

"Oooooo."

"Rather reminded me of Sandor-Xo!"

"Ooooooo."

"I should have shown him my sword, I suppose!"

"Oooooo."

"The business end, I mean!"

"Oooooo. ... Oh Trazel! He was right! He didn't lie at the end. Because I *am* stupid! So stupid! So blind! And to think it was your guilelessness that saved us, Trazel! Believe me, I shall be grateful forever!"

"Don't even mention it."

"No. Listen to me! I think I know now why He made you as He did! Why He assigned you to me. It was to off-set my boundless ignorance! Oh Trazel, I am ashamed! Ashamed and grateful! I'm reminded I owe you a favor!"

"Oh forget the favor!"

"No! Never! Believe me when I say I am ready to make good on that favor whenever you want!"

"I need no favor, Karam-Bor. All I want is to get on with our mission."

"So do I. With all my heart. And the sooner the better!"

"Have we seen enough here?"

"For now."

"And where are we bound next?"

"To the Seventh Moon of Behazi."

"And we can leave soon?"

"Immediately."

Trazel drew the folds of his robe round him. He took one last look at the group of creatures standing about the mourning mother.

"Now that I've grown accustomed to seeing them," he said, "I'm not so sure they wouldn't make good candidates. The may look a bit *outré*. But certainly they are a caring lot."

"I wouldn't deny it," said Karam-Bor.

"I do hope Ramey-Do doesn't bump into us again."

"A hollow hope, I'm afraid. Ramey-Do knows we're around. He'll keep a close eye on us now. Let's hope the next time we'll be ready for him."

CHAPTER 7
The Seventh Moon of Behazi

More swiftly than light they journeyed through the corridors of space until at last they reached the light force Olanthros-Tau.

This star, like nearly all others they passed, held a score of whirling captives under its influence. One of them, Behazi as it was called, was considerably larger than the others, holding under its own power eleven moons. The cloud-enwrapped seventh, their destination, appeared from afar like a soft ball of whitest cotton.

At a point just above the moon's surface, they paused while Karam-Bor began to rummage through the information packet.

"Now let's see what we have here," he murmured.

He fingered one sheet of paper after another until he came up with one crammed with columns of figures. After squinting at them awhile, he said: "According to these tables, the moon is reaching the end of its period of exposure to the light force. Soon it will pass into the shadow of Behazi."

"And what does that mean?" Trazel asked.

"Quite simply that a long cold night is about to set in. The temperature is going to drop. Drop abruptly. When that happens, the clouds which surround the moon will change to snow. The snow will fall until the sky overhead turns as clear as diamond. At the same time, the water will have begun to freeze. Within seven of their days, the moon's surface will be a solid crust of snow and ice. Only in its deepest parts will the sea remain unfrozen."

"A remarkable transformation!" exclaimed Trazel.

"A rather vicious transformation, all things considered. A whole change of worlds!"

"And how long will it remain in its snowball stage?"

Karam Bor studied the data sheet.

"According to these figures, the Seventh Moon of Behazi remains frozen for a period of forty-seven revolutions. At that point it emerges once more from the shadow of Behazi back into the warming rays of Olanthros-Tau. The process then reverses itself. The ice and snow begin to melt. The waters warm. Sea plants sprout and grow quickly. Along the equator the water heats to the boiling point, sending up vast quantities of steam which become a thickening layer of clouds throughout the light phase. And so it goes. Freeze and thaw. Thaw and freeze."

"And the creatures we've been sent to investigate?"

Karam-Bor began riffling pages once more. At last he came up with two sheets clipped together and marked at the top: POTENTIAL BEINGS OF CHOICE / THE SEVENTH MOON OF BEHAZI.

"They are called," said Karam-Bor, reading and speaking at the same time, "Kelyds. Ah ... of moderate size. Average of eleven and twelve to the third power, omicron waves — "

He read on silently.

"Hmmmm. Omnivorous. Monogamous. Long-lived in comparison to other creatures in the moon's waters. ... Yes, and it says here: 'Their intelligence approaches the power of samek on the mem-lamed scale, a development due in part to the sequence of extreme cold and extreme warmth in which they are obliged to live. This very adversity has brought about great development of spirit and mind. The Kelyds have learned to turn their difficulties to their advantage. As an example, they have devised a way of diverting boiling water during the light phase into a storage area where it is kept for the duration of the freeze. This procedure permits them to remain fairly close to the surface throughout the darkness phase, living in pockets of warmth. At the same time, they know how to divert the cold water of the depths upward to cool them when their dwelling place becomes overly warm."

"How do they nourish themselves during their winter?"

"Apparently they have developed simple methods of preserving food."

"Still, I should think they would dread their night."

"On the contrary. They seem to look forward to it. According to this data sheet, it is, for them, a time for leisure, for music, for enjoying each others' company."

"I suppose they are able to predict when the day ends and the night begins."

"Indeed they are. Here it says they've learned simple forms of calculation. They tell time during the hot phase by the slant of the rays of Olanthros-Tau."

"And when it is dark?"

"By observing the development of the ice."

"And is it such intelligence that brings them close to the power of choice?"

"Not entirely. Their primary credentials, according to our information, come from a curious sense of joy. They live under extremely difficult and dangerous conditions. Yet they are happy. They sing a good deal. They rarely fret. It is almost as though they sense a certain blessedness at the center of things."

"I can't imagine more appropriate guests," mused Trazel.

"That seems to be the consensus back in Operations, as you know. Still, we can't go about making choices until we've investigated all possibilities."

"Then why don't we get on with it?"

"As you say, Trazel, why don't we?"

Down through the clouds which concealed the moon they

darted. At their base they found a sphere entirely covered with water. In equatorial regions the surface of the moon was boiling away furiously in the furnace-like heat of Olanthros-Tau, sending up great sheets of steam into the atmosphere which swirled about and formed new clouds.

In the more temperate zones, halfway to the poles, the temperature had sufficiently moderated to allow a dense vegetation to grow in the water.

The first living beings they came upon beneath the surface of the water proved to be a herd of large, grey, docile-looking creatures grazing upon sea vegetation. These moved placidly through the water by means of paddle-shaped appendages which ended in horn-like barbs for self-protection.

Not far off roamed a pack of flesh-eaters, long and sleek as rapiers. With huge eyes and dish-like depressions for hearing — the sensory apparatus which enabled them to go on hunting in the darkness of the long night — they glided slowly about, ever alert for stragglers from the herd.

The sea grazers paid little heed. So long as they kept close together the predators posed no danger. Their primary function at this time was to consume huge quantities of sea greenery which would sustain them throughout the period of hibernation about to begin.

As Karam-Bor and Trazel were observing the grazers and their predators, there came from afar sounds of music. The melody had a rising and falling character, rather like a strange, haunting keen. As the form of the melody became apparent, it began to be interwoven by a second melody, and then a third in a delicate counterpoint.

Despite the eerie beauty of the music, the sea grazers turned restive. They ceased feeding and began to herd more closely together.

As for the flesh eaters, their movements quickened, as though aware of opportunities to come. Darting and turning, they flashed the white undersides of their bellies. Opened mouths revealed arrays of glittering, rasp-like teeth.

Soon there swam into view three sea creatures. Karam-Bor and Trazel sensed an immediate kinship. Clearly these were Kelyds, the Potential Beings of Choice they sought. Nor was it so much their appearance which revealed their identity, but rather an aura of self-awareness. For these were not one with the grazers or the predators, compelled primarily by instinct. Instead they were creatures able to assess consciously their aims, and to go after them in a deliberate manner.

Their bodies were well-adapted to the environment. The head was clearly defined and equipped with enormous dark and limpid eyes. The flippers which propelled them were long and slender, and possessed not only remarkable powers of axis, but ended in finger-like projections capable of grasping.

With these fingers, the creatures dragged behind them a net fabricated of sea vines. They sang as they moved — their singing a form of communication, so that their conversation had the quality of an elaborate fugue.

When they spotted the herd, the Kelyds stopped and sang to each other their songs of strategy.

The sea grazers, meanwhile, had retreated into an area of dense sea vegetation. Large, bullish leaders of the herd positioned themselves in its vanguard, emitting menacing grunts. One actually charged the hunters, though its rush was too clumsy to be a genuine threat.

It was when the hunters began to deploy their net that the herd panicked. Wild roars of alarm sounded, as the creatures thrashed about in a terrified rush for distance. Some of the smaller sea grazers, confused and terrified by the watery stampede, darted off by themselves, and were promptly set upon by waiting predators, who devoured them in a frenzy.

In the meantime, the hunters had spread their net and begun the process of isolating a small group of the fully-

grown creatures. With great skill they maneuvered these
away from the others.

The sea grazers' initial concern was to avoid the net. Then
suddenly aware that they had become separated from the
others, they became confused. A few bewildered turns to gain
their bearings, and they made a dash for the herd.

All avoided the net save one.

The creature struggled powerfully to be free. The net
bulged, and in places actually burst as the grazer wallowed
violently against its restraints.

Working together, the hunters held the net secured. Their
tactic was to keep the prey enclosed until it tired.

And gradually fatigue did overtake the beast. And when
this had become apparent, one of the Kelyds released his hold
on the net and retrieved a sharpened rod which had been left
in a sea vine. Holding the rod in its rudimentary fingers, the
hunter returned and slowly began to circle the netted prey,
looking for an opening.

Then a sudden swoop, and the rod had been thrust deeply
into the grazer's body.

Once more the creature began to thrash about, this time in
a greater frenzy than ever. Only now its blood had begun to
dye the waters. Soon it weakened. A final convulsion, and the
hunt was over.

With their prey still enmeshed in the net, the Kelyds began
to swim back in the direction from which they had come.

Karam-Bor and Trazel followed.

A considerable distance was traversed before the rock-
ledged sea floor below them began to slope upward, forming
a marine ridge. The waters here turned warmer. Not far overhead could be seen the seething surface of the Seventh Moon
of Behazi.

The ridge arose toward the perpendicularity of a cliff. In
the face of the cliff there appeared an opening.

The Kelyds with their prey swam through the opening. Karam-Bor and Trazel came after them.

Inside they found themselves in a capacious underwater cavern lighted by globes of phosphorescent seaweed.

The interior was arranged like a primitive village. A part of the cavern had been given over to sleeping quarters. Yet another section was set aside for the storage and preparation of food. Nearer at hand lay a communal area.

The waters of the cavern were cooled by the flow of an icy gush of water diverted from the depths. These same waters would be warmed during the long frigid night about to descend from a cistern-like enclosure of extremely hot water siphoned down from the surface. The cistern lay along one side of the cavern.

The hunters had already sung forth their arrival. Scores of other Kelyds soon appeared from the various parts of the dwelling and helped drag the catch to a circle of rocks at the center of the communal area. There the creatures began a chorus of thanksgiving both sung and danced in a slow, formal rhythm.

When the rite was completed, some of those present dragged the carcass of the sea-grazer to the rear of the cavern, where they dismembered it with knives of sharpened rock. The pieces of flesh were plunged into the hot water of the cistern, then stored in fissures in the cavern walls.

Meanwhile, other Kelyds had begun the preparation of a meal composed of both flesh food and sea greenery. When ready, all members of the clan gathered and together keened a melody before partaking of the food.

After observing these various activities, Trazel commented: "I must say, I don't like their custom of killing other creatures in order to eat. But beyond that, I find them rather to my liking."

"They certainly do seem to treat one another with every

consideration," said Karam Bor. "And excellent manners besides! Excellent!"

"Are there other clans of Kelyds on this sphere?"

"Many."

"And how does one clan get along with another?"

"Rather nicely, it seems. According to the data in the
packet, they're not above fighting over hunting territories.
But in general, Kelyds have a way of getting along together fairly well."

"I suppose we should visit some of these other clans to
verify the information. Don't you agree, Karam-Bor?"

Karam-Bor replied that he was about to make the same
suggestion himself. And so the two began a leisurely tour of
the Seventh Moon of Behazi, visiting this group of Kelyds
and that. And they found every situation much like the first.
The sea creatures without exception were gentle, intelligent,
happy beings who in the midst of a harsh sequence of living
conditions had created for themselves a peaceful, pleasant existence.

So engrossed were they in their sight-seeing that Karam-
Bor and Trazel quite forgot about Ramey-Do. There had
been no sign of the Fallen One anywhere. And so, without
thinking about it, they assumed he'd simply gone off to some
other spot in the Circle of Becoming to stir up trouble.

By the time they completed their circuit of the moon and
had returned to the first colony of Kelyds they'd encountered, the moon had begun to slip into the shadow of Behazi.

Almost immediately the air over the sea took chill; and in a
jolting confrontation with the warmth of the sea, it became
transformed into a wild, violent blizzard of global proportions.

As the wind-driven snow swirled about the surface of the
moon, and a crust of ice began to form across the face of the
waters, the various sea creatures began a descent to the

depths where they would be safe. Before three moon days had passed, the sphere lay locked in the darkness and cold of its unrelenting winter.

In the cavern, the pace of the Kelyds began to slow. The waters above them, which had been boiling furiously only a few days before, now began to congeal into ice. Little by little the layer of ice thickened and descended until at last it came to rest upon the roof of the cavern. For a time there came great sounds of creaking and groaning as the weight of the ice built up pressure. Meanwhile, the water all about the cavern began to freeze until, at last, the entire cavern was sealed off.

The Kelyds seemed undismayed by their entrapment. They gathered in groups to partake of stored provisions. Some whiled away the time with singing. Some repaired nets. Some engaged in the elaborate ritual of mating. Some gave birth to new Kelyds.

And so the life of these sea creatures continued in their prison of ice, all of them sustained by the heated waters of the cistern and the food which had been stored away.

Nothing that Karam-Bor or Trazel could detect altered their belief that these were, by any standard, the most likely new additions to the guest list of the Banquet. At one point, Trazel went so far as to suggest that they issue the invitation at once. Karam-Bor responded with a smile of forebearance and a remark to the effect that while he could well understand the reasons for such an impulse, it still remained necessary for them to visit all of the Potential Spheres of Operative Choice before reaching a final decision.

It was when they were about to leave for their third assignment that disaster struck the colony.

Pressure from the ice formation caused a crack to develop in the hot water containment area. The Kelyds made frantic efforts to seal it off. Some became badly burned in the attempt. But to no avail. The fissure widened. Gradually the heated water leached out against the wall of ice where it too began to freeze.

As the interior temperature in the cavern dropped, the creatures did their best to deal with a situation which they perceived as hopeless. Mothers hovered about the young, reassuring them with soft singing. Certain of the larger Kelyds attempted to chop a hole in the ice of the inlet which, during the hot season, brought cold water up from below, all in a futile attempt to provide an escape to the safety of the deep.

Karam-Bor and Trazel looked on helplessly as shards of ice began to form on the cavern ceiling and walls. Gradually the creatures became paralyzed with cold.

But, then, as death seemed imminent, a curious event took place.

One of the Kelyds detached himself from the others and swam toward the two. As it drew near, a song came forth — a lovely lament in which the sea creature sang of its awareness of the presence of the two beings from the Kingdom of Light. This was followed by an appeal for help. If Trazel could but draw his fire-edged sword, the Kelyd sang, the inlet could be cleared of ice, and the clan make its escape to the unfrozen waters below.

Trazel turned excitedly to Karam-Bor.

"Why didn't I think of that before?"

"Perhaps because it is not allowed," the elder replied sadly. "You know we can't intrude upon the circumstances which provide these creatures with their freedom."

"But this has nothing to do with freedom, Karam-Bor! It's their *lives* we're concerned with now! You see them suffering, don't you? Even the little ones! They tremble with the cold! They are terrified, Karam-Bor! Soon they shall die! I should think that freedom has no meaning, what with survival at stake!"

"Freedom is a greater boon than survival," said Karam-Bor softly. "There is no greater good than freedom."

"Not even life itself?"

"Not even life itself."

"I can't believe that, Karam-Bor! I won't believe it!"

"Trazel, I feel as badly as you. I weep for these lovely creatures. I do not want to see them perish any more than you do. But, we cannot — we simply cannot intrude on their misfortunes!"

"But such a small thing! A turn of a blade, and a good deed is done!"

"Ah, but many a kindness has been a terrible betrayal to Him, I fear. No, Trazel. As much as we might want to, we cannot assist these beings. When the time comes, I'm afraid we shall have to issue the invitation to some other clan."

The lone Kelyd began to sing once more. His appeal was now made directly to Trazel. He cried that the novice's courage and power were the only hope left to the sufferers now. If he could but grant this one request, could but draw his sword, the name of Trazel would be revered forever among the Kelyds."

The thought pleased Trazel. He contemplated the various satisfactions of being regarded as a savior. And such, he told himself, he could be! All it required was a few deft thrusts of his fiery weapon!

Disregarding everything Karam-Bor had told him, he reached for the jasper handle at his side. As he began to pull the blade from its holder, the fire along its edge caused the icy water to bubble and steam. In the turbulence he lost sight of Karam-Bor. Nor did he care by then! The important thing was to free the Kelyds before it was too late!

But then, with the blade halfway out, he felt the elder's powerful grip over his own, forcing the sword back into its scabbard. Nor was there any resisting the superior force of

Karam-Bor.

And when the froth and mist all around him began to clear, he could see that it would have been too late anyway. The colony of Kelyds lay motionless in adamantine ice.

Nevertheless, the one Kelyd remained — the one who had made an appeal to his mercy. And it was only after he'd stared awhile into the depthless, inky fury of the creature's eyes that he recognized the presence of Ramey-Do. And even after the Kelyd body assumed by the Fallen One began to disappear, the hate-filled gaze lingered.

"It was him all along!" gasped Trazel.

"So it was."

"You must have known!"

"I can't say I did, Trazel. In fact, much as I hate to admit it, my reaction was more a matter of luck than anything else. All I wanted to do was keep you from flouting my authority."

"I'm glad for that."

"I guess I am too."

"You know, Karam-Bor, it was just as Sandor-Xo said. He made his appeal to my highest ideals!"

"It's often the case."

"And I believed him with all my heart."

"They're very clever when it comes to causes."

"I suppose we'll meet up with him again — "

"We'd better not forget it."

"And he will tempt us as before — "

"I'm not so sure," said Karam-Bor. He mulled over the matter for a time. Then he said, "First he tried his wiles on me. Next he tried them on you. I wouldn't be surprised if the next time he'll have a go at those whom we choose."

CHAPTER 8
Eden

The sphere was somewhat larger than the Seventh Moon of Behazi, though considerably smaller than either of the Twin Captives. It lay towards the outskirts of the light cluster, floating serenely in the void, its surface a swirling mixture of white and blue.

Karam-Bor and Trazel descended to its surface and began a leisurely circuit, passing over the poles.

The richness and variety of living things far surpassed anything they had encountered so far. Against the intense whiteness of the polar caps they saw bear and wolves, seals and walrus. The oceans which spread forth from the ice teemed with sea life. Presiding over all were the lordly whales, abundant and magnificent in their watery pastures.

Over water and land, birds skated the winds — winds fresh and clean as the first dawn.

The land which shouldered its way out of the water lay rich and green under a molten sun. Lowlands formed random patterns of prairie and forest, while uplands thrust skyward toward peaks ablaze with snow and sun.

Rivers ran pure. The streams which fed them seemed strewn with diamonds, so brilliantly they threw back the beams from the light force.

"How lovely it all is!" Trazel cried, quite overcome by the exquisite beauty of the sphere. "It has the best of the other two worlds, doesn't it, Karam-Bor? I mean there is land in all shapes and colors, and there is water besides! A kind of duet for the eyes!

"Not half bad," admitted Karam-Bor. He frowned as he said so, adding, "But remember what Sandor-Xo told us! The Potential Beings of Choice here are the most troublesome of the lot!"

"Yes, so I recall. But have you discovered what's wrong with them?"

"All I remember is that they're self-centered to a remarkable degree — far more than they need for survival. It makes them ever so quarrelsome and disagreeable! In fact, they can turn quite murderous at times!"

"How sad! Really! To live in such beauty, and to be so fretful."

"'Tis a pity, no doubt of it."

"Tell me, Karam-Bor, do these creatures live in water or on land?"

Karam-Bor, who'd already begun to extract sheafs of paper from the information packet, found the data sheet and quickly scanned it.

"According to our information," he said after a moment or two, "they began their existence in water. Then, by degrees, they transferred their arrangements to land."

"Do they look watery, or landish?"

"More landish than watery. And not, sad to say, all that attractive in any event. But let me give you the official description. 'Homo Erectus. Oxygenous. Omnivorous. Polygamous. Presently this creature inhabits the rain forests of the largest land mass. The Potential Being of Choice in question is of moderate size — fourteen to the fourth power, sigma wavelength. Its basic configuration is as follows: a central body mass, with two hinged appendages below for purposes of mobility, two similar appendages above for grasping and climbing. Connected to the central body mass is a separate case, or head, somewhat round of appearance, which contains two organs of vision, moderate perception. The case also contains two noise collectors, as well as a curious protuberance for purposes of oxygenation as well as detecting scents. Also there is an opening for ingesting food and water, beside which there is a relatively large thought apparatus — resh, on the mem-lamed scale."

"It would seem they think well enough. But I'm afraid they won't be a treat for our eyes!"

"Worse than the Versidians with their two heads, I wouldn't be surprised! But don't forget what I told you. Thanks to Him who sits at the Head Table, such as these would be properly bodied and clothed before they came within hailing distance of the Banquet, were they invited to attend."

"Yes, and I remember something else you told me. You said that they look all right to one another."

"Let us devoutly hope so."

"But what makes these creatures prospects for the Banquet, Karam-Bor?"

"The usual. Rudimentary thinking, to begin with. Matter of survival, don't you see. They found themselves too puny to fight for their place under the light force. Nor were they quick enough to flee their predators. And so the organ of their cleverness began to expand. It was a case of learning to outwit ones' foes, or be eaten by them. The rest followed. They learned to tether the power of fire. They discovered the secret of seed and growth. They even began to tame certain of the lesser animals."

"Karam-Bor, I can't imagine that we will ever choose to issue the Invitation to such as these. That being the case, what will happen to them?"

"They will grow more clever at outwitting the others with whom they share the world. Soon they will over-run it. In so doing, they will destroy it. It's what comes of being clever without being wise."

While he'd been speaking, Karam-Bor had taken once more to shuffling through the information packet. What he wanted was the chart which indicated the way to the area inhabited by the Potential Beings of Choice.

In order to set his course, Karam-Bor was required to triangulate two stars and the light force. Grumbling that he'd never been very good at geometry, he set off for the largest land mass on the sphere. Trazel followed close behind. In something less than an instant they found themselves on the border of a great rain forest.

The various creatures here seemed to sense their presence, for upon their arrival a strange pause overtook the movements and sound of the forest. Birds, which just a moment before had been whistling and ratcheting, grew silent. Monkeys stopped their chattering. Gazelles and antelope stood paralyzed in the high grass at the edge of the forest as they sniffed the wind. Leopards edged back into their camouflage and, with huge amber eyes, studied the near vicinity. Lizards froze onto the sides of rocks. Snakes glided into bushes and lay there as motionless as the sinuous roots all around them.

Karam-Bor and Trazel moved deeper into the midday twilight of the rain forest until they came upon a stream which had been dammed by a pile of rocks. Leading away from the dam was a footpath.

The two followed it until they arrived at a simple fortification. Saplings dug into the ground formed a semi-circle around a yard space. On the far side of the yard a cliff rose up in which lay the openings to a number of caves.

The enclosed area had been trampled down into a mud crust. At its center stood a great pole with carvings on it, and a smokey fire at its base.

The collection of creatures who inhabited the compound were busy at various tasks. Some hacked away at firewood with stone axes. Others pounded tubers, stone on stone, to a paste. Still other were in the process of dismembering a horse-like creature with vivid black and white markings. A part of the process involved removing the creature's skin, a task carried out with the use of small rocks which had been chipped to a fine edge. The purpose to which the skin would be put was evident enough, for the members of the clan had wrapped pieces of it about their feet. Outside of this and a few bright bird feathers worn in the hair, the creatures wore nothing at all.

At the entrances to the caves, a number of the smaller creatures played with pebbles and sticks. Beyond, in the shadows, lay a heap of dead creatures awaiting dismemberment — a gazelle, a sloth, and also a creature who was clearly like those of the clan, a Homo Erectus.

"Oh dear, I'm afraid they've gone and slain one of their own," said Trazel.

"But not a member of their particular clan," replied Karam-Bor. He pointed to the feather lodged in the hair of the corpse. It was of a different color than those worn by the creatures in the enclosure.

"I suppose they'll dine on him," said Trazel, unable to repress a shudder.

"With relish, I fear. Somewhere in the data it says that they are much given to this sort of thing."

While they had been observing the group, the light force had climbed to the point where it hovered almost directly overhead. The hotness and humidity of the rain forest approached midday intensity. Work at the various tasks languished, as creatures began to arrange themselves in a semi-circle upwind of the fire.

For a time they ate, chewing and snarling over the raw flesh of animals. Handfuls of the paste from the mashed tubers and a few berries completed the meal. Water for drinking came from a skin hanging inside one of the caves.

When sated, the creatures divided into smaller groups. The older, more powerful men, those who were warriors and hunters, gathered about them the women and children claimed as their own. What remained of the clan were but a few male adolescents. As potential challengers to the older men, they were required to keep off by themselves.

Gradually the members of the clan composed themselves to rest. Snores began to fill the air.

But not all of them, Karam-Bor and Trazel could see, had gone to sleep. Two remained awake. Of these, one was a young man kept separate from the group. When sure the others were asleep, he began to act out the progress of a hunt. With a stick for a spear, he pretended to find and stalk an animal. At times he would play the part of a hunter. At other times he was the hunted.

The pantomime was carried out very quietly, but with great drama; for the young man was not presenting this bit of theatrics for his own benefit. Rather, another member of the clan remained awake while the others slept away the heat of the day. She was young and remarkably pretty. The marks of her womanhood were only just beginning to bud. She had long straight black hair which framed a rather delicate oval face in which were set two large, dark, fawn-like eyes.

Shyly she watched the young man play out his drama. That there was already something of a conspiracy between them was made evident by the quick looks the actor threw in her direction. She, in turn, observed his antics from the corners of admiring eyes. And when at last he made a particularly bold maneuver, she could not suppress a loud giggle.

The sound stirred the grizzled old warrior who lay close by. This man had recently claimed the maiden as his own, confident that she would bear him many children.

His eyes opened. Had he heard what he though he heard?

His head raised. He looked around.

All who were held under his protection seemed soundly asleep. Nothing unusual, he assured himself. Perhaps he'd been dreaming.

Gradually he gave himself back over to sleep.

The young man had been watching all the while from beneath lowered lids. When certain that the old man was asleep once more, he resumed the drama. And once more the beautiful young maiden encouraged him with her eyes until he grew bolder and bolder, and at last elicited from her another giggle.

The old warrior caught it, only this time remained as before, pretending to sleep. He let his ears sort out the sounds all around him. And when they reached a particular stage, he lunged upright.

There was no mistaking the situation. After all, the young males were always after the young females. It was a part of the life of the clan. And when it happened, lessons had to be taught.

With a growl coming from deep within his throat and a showing of teeth, the old warrior advanced on his challenger. The youth, in turn, scurried to a place of safety near the fence.

The elder, who was stronger but not quicker than his adversary, turned instead upon the maiden. Catching her by one arm, he pummeled her severely.

She wept silently, lest her cries double the old man's fury. When he'd finished her punishment, he threw her roughly to the ground. Turning, he surveyed the yard. The young man cowered in its furthest corner.

Confident he'd put an end to these annoyances, the old man settled himself, and soon gave over to sleep once more.

The young woman had gone on crying softly, rubbing her bruised body. Her hurt at length drew the youth nearer. He tried to comfort her with his eyes. And when this failed, he edged closer still until at last he was able to reach out and touch her arm.

Her response was to lean toward him and press her head against his shoulder.

They might have gone undetected, had not an animal outside the compound taken that very moment to step on a dry branch and snap it in two.

The warriors, trained to danger, awakened in an instant. The old one, who had claimed the maiden, once more took in the status of things.

With a roar of rage, he sprang at the couple. A swing of the forearm caught the young man in the side of the head, knocking him to the ground and leaving him stunned. The warrior turned and caught up his spear. He began to circle the youth, shrieking his complaint to the gathering clan, so that they would know why he was about to kill blood kin.

Slowly he raised his spear. The others, meanwhile, had begun to scream — screeching out their excitement, their horror, and yet, curiously, their approval too. The young man was obliged to die! He'd broken the code of clan behavior! The warrior circling him with raised spear had every right to run him through!

And he would have done so, had not the maiden reached out to implore him. Clutching at one leg, she only managed to push it behind the other. Down the old man fell, the rock-tipped spear skittering free.

The young man by now had fully regained his senses. He saw the old man face down in the dust. He saw the spear rolling towards him.

Terror brought recklessness. It took but a moment — a moment to scramble to his feet, a moment to grasp the spear, a moment to drive it deeply into the old man's back. Then, catching the maiden by the wrist, he darted out of the compound. Together the two plunged into the underbrush.

Panic fueled them. They ran a dodging aimless course, their only intent to be free of their pursuers.

As it turned out, the only ones to come after them were Karam-Bor and Trazel, who wondered what might become of the two.

When exhaustion overcame the young man and woman, they threw themselves under a thick bush and, disregarding the thorns and their labored breathing, listened for the cracking and pounding of oncoming footsteps. But the only sounds they heard were the familiar noises of the rain forest.

Soon after, as if they had quite forgotten the violence which had brought them here, the young man resumed his pantomime. Only now the maiden watched and applauded openly. And after awhile, she arose and took the part of the hunted, while he stalked her with as much seriousness as their laughter would allow.

When they had their fill of pantomime, they began to stroll through the forest. They found water to drink and berries to eat. And in a while they discovered a blanket of soft grass to lie upon.

They spoke with each other — their language a blend of throat sounds, gestures and grimaces. But when the lad pulled the girl closer and attempted to embrace her, she was on her feet in an instant with the lightest, softest shriek imaginable, and darted away as though a wisp of cottonwood seed.

He pursued her. But she was incredibly nimble and could not be caught. And when, made breathless with running and hilarity, they stopped and looked at one another, it was with an unutterable longing.

All this while the light force had been dropping lower and lower into the trees; and what had previously been a dappled rain forest now began to settle back into a uniform shade.

The advent of darkness robbed them of their light-heartedness, as they began to wonder where they might hide from the terrible night to come.

Came at last a place in the forest where they could turn one way or another. The young man had already made up his mind. But when he went to tell his companion, he saw that she was not looking at him. Rather, her soft doe's eyes, widened in astonishment, seemed to be gazing past him.

He turned.

Not far from where they stood could be seen a blaze of light. An open place, he thought, in the forest. Perhaps they had reached the great meadow near their home.

At the same time it occurred to him that the old warrior might be dead. If so, they would be accepted back into the clan. If not, the young man would be obliged to fight him to the death. Either way it was better than remaining alone in the rain forest when the light force failed.

The maiden, as though mesmerized, brushed past the young man and ran toward the brightness.

He followed.

Down through a glen and over a rise they sauntered. And then all at once the two, for the first time in their lives, stepped out of the rain forest — stepped into the unimpeded domain of a late afternoon sun.

They stood there in bewilderment, gazing at a world which had been spoken of by some of the bravest warriors, but of which they themselves knew nothing. There before them lay a vast savanna — an enormous ocean of grass which extended to a point at the limit of sight where, each day, the light force rose.

Their astonishment gradually turned to dread. Where could they be? To what awesome place had they come?

Wherever, it was much too far from the center of the earth, too far from that point symbolized by the pole which stood in the midst of the clan enclosure.

And yet, it was not only the sense of being far from the center of their being that overwhelmed them; it was also the experience of being so suddenly thrust into a new and unimaginable world. And even as they gazed at that world, the sun was turning the color of golden rose, and beginning to slide down behind the trees.

Too terror-stricken to advance into the savanna, a similar terror kept them from returning to the darkness of the forest.

A lone tree stood a ways out in the savanna. It seemed to offer the only possible relief. What was more, they could see fruit nestled among it leaves.

Hesitantly they moved toward it. Timidly they ate of the fruit. Then they began to make for themselves a place of concealment beneath its branches — a shelter from the advancing night.

CHAPTER 9
An Invitation to a Banquet

Trazel had found himself overwhelmed with pity for the young couple. And yet it was a pity seasoned by fascination. For reasons he could not begin to fathom, he'd become enchanted by the two — marveling at their recklessness, their unaccountable happiness, their limitless attraction to one another.

"Karam-Bor," he said, as he watched the two prepare a place for themselves under the fruit tree. "How did they manage to get themselves into such a terrible predicament — all that blood and misery and mayhem? And now they're lost to boot!"

"It's all on account of passion," replied Karam-Bor gruffly.

"And yet we've watched them play and laugh the afternoon away as though it would never end. How could they do that?"

"Passion."

"And why, even now with the darkness upon them, do they go on looking into each others' eyes? Why?"

"Passion," said Karam-Bor, adding with a soupcon of disgust, "and a totally illicit passion at that, as you've no doubt noticed."

"When he tries to hold her, she runs away. What is the reason for that?"

"Passion."

"Then, as soon as he stops trying, she sighs and looks sad. Why?"

"Passion," declared Karam-Bor. "Passion, passion, passion. Nothing but passion."

"And what are they doing now?" Trazel asked.

"They ... they've fallen asleep."

"What is that — sleep?"

"It is ... forgetting. It's dying a little. It's dreaming. All of those things, and more."

"And why should the creatures of the Circle of Becoming fall, as you say, asleep?"

"Partly because they fear the darkness. Darkness is as death to them."

"What is it like to die, Karam-Bor?"

"It is like falling asleep. Only in such a case you never wake up. You sink forever into the Everlasting Darkness."

"But on the other hand you could go to the Banquet!"

"Yes. Providing you receive an invitation. That, and choose to go."

By now the stars had taken on a brilliant intensity against the Everlasting Darkness. Nocturnal beasts of prey began to patrol the edge of the forest. Karam-Bor and Trazel could see them quite clearly, even though they, in turn, remained invisible. None ventured close to the pair for a long time. But then a great, lean tiger caught their scent, and, following it, padded to within a few paces of them.

Trazel decided to unsheath his sword.

Its flame exploded in the darkness. Snarling and hissing its fear, the tiger broke for the forest.

"I must warn you again against unwarranted interference in the Circle of Becoming," said Karam-Bor severely.

"I'm sorry, Karam-Bor," said Trazel, abashed. "My sword was out of its scabbard before I thought much about it."

"Well, no harm done. As you can see, they slept through it all."

"I'm so glad they did. I mean, what a turn it would have

given them to wake up and find a huge, stripey beast sniffing at their toes. And yet," Trazel added reflectively, as he gazed at the heavens above him, "I could almost wish they were awake now, so they could fill their eyes with the stars!"

"I doubt they've ever seen so many at once, living under trees as they have."

"So wonderful, His fireworks! So splendid!"

"It's not a sight you soon tire of," Karam-Bor agreed, allowing his mood to mellow.

"I never will. I promise!"

"You know, Trazel, it wasn't so long ago that we were far off in the midst of them. Do you have any idea where?"

"None at all. I was content to follow where you led."

"Would you like to know?"

"Most certainly!"

"Then look directly overhead where the cluster is thickest."

"Yes?"

"See if you can make out two large fragments which almost seem to touch one another. ... There! Where I'm pointing!"

"I think I see them."

"Just below you'll find five smaller ones."

"In a kind of ragged line?"

"That's it. That's where I want you to look! Because, Trazel, the second from the top was our first stop. That particular point of light is Capal-Resh."

"So far away?"

"Not next door, by any means."

"And where is the light force that rules the Seventh Moon of Behazi?"

"Olanthros-Tau. ... It's under the horizon. You can't see it from here."

"Do you suppose it has begun to shine once more on the moon, melting its ice?"

"Not yet, I'm afraid. But it won't be long."

"It makes me sad when I think of those poor Kelyds freezing as they did."

"Not a happy occasion, I grant you."

"As least there are other colonies of them."

"Oh yes! A healthy population, no doubt of it!"

"I must say, Karam-Bor, when we left the Seventh Moon of Behazi, I'd quite made up my mind that those wonderful creatures of the sea would be my choice."

"My sentiments as well. The Kelyds are precisely the sort of guests we want for the Banquet."

"Not that I have anything against those gentle green creatures on the Twin Captives."

"Nor I. They had many qualities to recommend them."

"But what about these?" Trazel asked, indicating the pair asleep in each others' arms. "What is your opinion of them?"

Karam-Bor permitted himself an indulgent smile.

"Oh, they're all right, I suppose. Still they run a poor third in my book. Not that they're totally beyond redemption, understand. It ... It's ... Well, it's just that they're not our sort."

"How do you mean that?"

"I'm not sure I know how to put it, Trazel, without sounding conceited. All I would say is they're a little too crabby, a little too vicious to suit me. Always wanting something that isn't theirs! All too ready to turn nasty if they don't get it! I mean, you saw yourself what those two there are capable of! That's why I have no compunctions whatever in crossing them off the list."

Trazel remained silent a few moments.

"I know you're right, Karam-Bor," he said at length. "These creatures *do* have a mean streak, no doubt of it! And the Kelyds are quite wonderful! They're peaceable. They're generous. They're filled with music, and all that. But, I don't know. When I look down on the two of them under the tree there, I see the promise of something that is quite appealing. And ... well, to state the matter briefly, there's something inside me that says I ought to choose them!"

"*Them?*" said Karam-Bor, aghast.

Trazel nodded.

"As your first choice?"

Trazel nodded again, adding, "My first and only choice."

Karam-Bor considered this surprising development in silence for quite some time. Then abruptly he laughed.

"I know now, Trazel! This is your idea of a practical joke!"

"No, I assure you, Karam-Bor. I'm quite serious."

"Quite?"

"Ever so."

"Oh come now, Trazel! You know as well as I do that if we were to choose such as these we'd be the laughing stock of the entire Kingdom."

"Of course I'm used to being laughed at."

"But ... But they're ... they're ... they're *impossible*, Trazel! Absolutely impossible! You know yourself that we caught these two red-handed at treachery, at murder! Now how would you explain that up there?"

"I don't know. I'm not sure. Self-defense?"

"Self-*defense?* Why, that's ridiculous! I can think of no more flimsy reason in this world or any other! The fact is they were disobedient to the laws of their clan! The young female was pledged to the old man by customs of long standing. He was her protector. She owed her loyalty. Clearly those two there had no right to get into all that fol-de-rol that goes with mating!"

"But wouldn't you say they're more suited to one another?"

"Not the price of murder they aren't."

"At least you must feel a little sorry for them, out here all alone in a world they've never known!"

"What I feel is beside the point. The truth is they are the dupes of their own selfishness. And such selfishness has no place in the Kingdom!"

"Maybe they can change, Karam-Bor."

"It would take nothing less than a miracle!"

"But what will happen to them if we just go off and leave them?"

"They will die, of course. They cannot survive without the clan. It happens to be one of the major problems with this specimen. They can't live *with* one another. At the same time, they can't live *without* one another. So let's leave them with a hard lesson in the virtues of obedience and be on our way. By the time we get to the seventh Moon of Behazi, the ice will be gone."

"Please, let's stay just a while longer," Trazel pleaded.

Assured that the novice had overcome his stray impulse, Karam-Bor relented. They remained near the fruit tree until the night waned and the light force set the horizon beyond the savanna to smoldering.

The young man was the first to awaken. He looked about him in considerable amazement, as though surprised to find himself still alive.

The young woman rolled over onto her side, yawned and stretched. The youth regarded her tenderly, murmuring sounds of reassurance. But his reassurances became for her an alarm; for, remembering the conditions under which she'd gone to sleep, she violently pushed herself up and gazed wide-eyed at her surroundings: the savanna spreading out in one direction, and in the other the meandering wall of the rain forest.

Where was her home, with its warming fire, its food? What had become of her sisters and brothers and cousins? The loss of all that had been familiar set her sobbing.

The youth tried to comfort the maiden, even though he

himself trembled as much from fear as the dawn chill.

Trazel observed them awhile. Then suddenly he declared aloud: "No, I shan't be persuaded otherwise!"

"Be persuaded otherwise what, Trazel?"

"Be persuaded to give my choice to any but these!"

"To these? Are we back to that?"

"I'm sorry, Karam-Bor, but I *do* mean it! I know you're older and wiser than I. I know you regard them as the worst of the lot. And maybe they are! But since I've been given a choice all of my own, I choose *them* — him and her, those two there!"

"Oh glory! What a bother. What a nuisance!" muttered Karam-Bor to himself. "I should have known all along! I should have known he'd choose the least likely of all! Ah well." And so saying, he raised his voice to Trazel. "All right, my young friend. You go ahead and choose whomever you like! As for me, *I* choose the Kelyds! And, in case you're not aware of it, in the event of a division, the choice goes to the elder."

"And is that the end of it, Karam-Bor?"

"I'm pleased to say, it is! Make ready to return to the Seventh Moon of Behazi!"

"But haven't you forgotten something?"

"Forgotten something? And what could I have forgotten?"

"You've forgotten that ... that you owe me a favor."

These words jolted Karam-Bor into silence. He stood utterly motionless as he considered this information in all of its aspects. Then, at last, he said very quietly, "You wouldn't!"

"I'm afraid I would."

"You couldn't!"

"I'm afraid I could."

"You won't!"

"I'm afraid I will. ... After all, Karam-Bor, the idea of the favor was yours, not mine. And back there on the Twin Captives you urged me to make good on your promise whenever I liked. Well, Karam-Bor, I guess now is when I'd like to have the favor returned."

Karam-Bor gazed at the youth and the maiden with considerable distaste for a time. He then said: "Maybe we should discuss this awhile, Trazel."

"With all due respect, Karam-Bor, my mind is entirely made up. Entirely!"

"Trazel, listen! If we make these and all they represent our choice, we're going to have our hands full! You know yourself that we're obliged to remain here until the story is told. I'm warning you, unless you change your mind, you'll be driven mad by the likes of them. I guarantee it!"

Trazel decided he would not let himself be drawn into an argument. So he responded in a voice all honey and butter: "Let me tell you something interesting, Karam-Bor. Did you know that I am not even sure how the invitation is issued?"

"Oh, you're bound and determined, aren't you! You're not going to heed your elders! You're going to go your own way — just like those two there who insisted on their own way!"

"I mean, do you just say, 'Come to the Banquet!' or what?"

"Trazel, you're going to regret this day! Mark my words!"

"Or is it something written out?"

"All right! All right! I'm not going to welsh on my debts. I'll pay you your favor. But don't ever, ever say I didn't give you fair warning. And there's something else you can be sure of, my fresh young whirlagig. You'll be hearing me say 'I told you so!' for a good long time to come!"

Having punctuated these sentiments with a loud "Harrumph," Karam-Bor dug into the information packet. The first item to come forth was an instruction sheet relative to issuing the invitation.

After perusing it briefly, Karam-Bor explained to Trazel:

"It says here that we must first reveal ourselves to the two. So let me advise you, Trazel, if you think they were frightened before, it is as nothing compared to the shock they're about to get."

And indeed so. The youth and maiden reacted to the manifestation of Karam-Bor and Trazel with a paralyzing dread. The young man made a half-hearted effort to shield the young woman. But both mainly cowered, certain that they were about to die.

"Oh please don't be afraid!" Trazel called out solicitously. "We're not going to harm you!"

"You're wasting your words, Trazel," said Karam-Bor. "They're going to be frightened witless so long as they can see us, and that's all that can be said. 'Tis a mercy to state our business and let them get on with it."

"But will they understand you?"

"Not entirely. But they'll understand enough."

With these words, Karam-Bor laid aside the issuance material. Underneath lay an envelope wrought of finest gold. From it he withdrew a sheet of gold, beaten to a uniform fineness and folded in half. It was sealed with a dab of molten light, which shattered into a million sparks as Karam-Bor broke it.

"Ahem!" he declared to the couple, using his most official tone of voice. "I have a most important announcement to deliver to the two of you! Please do me the goodness of giving your utmost attention!"

The two cringed.

Karam-Bor held the invitation before him, cleared his throat and began to read.

"*To all persons to whom these presents may come, greeting. Be it known that you are hereby cordially invited to attend a Banquet given by Him who is the Creator of all.*"

"A very nice banquet," urged Trazel softly. "A lot of good things to eat and drink! None of that dreadful meat you've been ..."

"Please, Trazel! Please don't interrupt! They have enough of a problem listening to me! So be a good fellow and try to be quiet for now."

Karam-Bor returned his gaze to the sheet of gold.

"Now let's see. Where was I? Here!

'You will have a lifetime in which to respond to this invitation. Your time here is a time of choice. On the day your sojourn ends, you will have made that choice.'"

"There are the loveliest fireworks!" Trazel whispered to the two.

"Trazel! If you don't *mind*! We don't need a running commentary! All you do is make me lose my place! Where was I, anyway? Oh yes! Attend to me now, you two!

'With this power of choice you are raised to a new level of being. You are no longer merely one more created being on this sphere. Your bodies will, of course, remain akin to the creatures all around you. But inside there begins to come a difference. That difference centers in the power of choice, for you now have been endowed with the power to choose light or darkness, life everlasting or death everlasting, the food of heaven or the food of decay —'"

"Oh that food of heaven!" said Trazel, rubbing his stomach. "Yummmmmmy!"

"Trazel, I *implore* you!"

"Sorry, Karam-Bor."

"The invitation," Karam-Bor explained to the two, "ends with an RSVP. Is that clear?"

"They're planning to attend," said Trazel. "I'm sure of it!"

"That," Karam-Bor replied, "remains to be seen. But anyway, we might as well proceed to the final item of this business."

Karam-Bor fumbled through the papers of the information packet. Drawing forth an ordinary-looking sheet of paper, he scanned its contents.

"You there!" he called out sternly. "There's one more matter to be settled. So please listen carefully. To indicate your appetite for the Banquet to come, you are directed to refrain from eating an agreed-upon terrestrial food. It matters not what. A type of meat. A green. A fruit of some sort. ... Yes, like the fruit of the tree that shades you! That would do for a start. So then, let that fruit now become a test of your desire and your obedience! Do you understand?"

"They do, Karam-Bor!" said Trazel. "I'm sure of it! They won't take so much as a nibble! Believe me, they won't!"

"Such optimism." sighed Karam-Bor. To the two he said: "All right! That's all I have to say! You've got your invitation! Be off with you now! Find a place to settle down and begin to make up your minds about the Banquet. You have no further place in the rain forest. Your future is out there, toward the east. The forest that formed your life is forever closed to you."

Karam-Bor had no sooner spoken these words than a gorgeous, undulating creature appeared next to the two.

"What is that?" whispered Trazel.

"That, my friend, is a serpent," Karam-Bor whispered back. "But you might better ask, *who* is that? Because if you look closely, you'll see that it's none other than our old adversary, Ramey-Do."

"So it is! He showed up, just as you said he would!"

"And also just as I said, he's about to practice his wiles on our Beings of Choice."

"Dear me, I think he is at that, Karam-Bor! But what's the point of that curious body he's taken on?"

"Wisdom."

"Wisdom?"

"I'm afraid so. Our background data indicates that these beings somewhere got the idea that serpents are the very source and embodiment of all that is wise. It doesn't say how they came up with such insanity. All I can tell you is that they hold snakes in such reverence that they sometimes twine them on poles and hold them up to be adored."

"Karam-Bor! Look how eagerly they listen to what he has to say!"

And indeed, the couple had crept near to Ramey-Do and were now giving their closest attention.

"You poor darlings," Ramey-Do was telling them. "Treated so! Driven from your home! Frightened half out of your wits by these vagabonds! Sent packing God-knows-where! And if that weren't enough, they've gone and taken your *food* away! Not even a tiny morsel to sustain you! Why, it's hardly fair, if you ask me!"

"Karam-Bor, they're *listening* to him!" Trazel whispered urgently. "They're taking it all *in*!"

"It's starting already, I regret to say," Karam-Bor replied.

"What is starting?"

"A rebellion. A stupid, petty little rebellion. Slap-dashed together by two gullible creatures who inhabit a speck of nearly nothing halfway to nowhere. ... And Trazel, to think our choice would come to rest upon creatures who season their self-centeredness with violence! What a *dreadful* combination!"

"They hang on every *word* !"

"Really! Hardly the invitation out of my mouth, and they're trafficking in lies."

Karam-Bor broke off and called out severely: "Here, you two! Don't listen to the likes of him! You'll be getting into more trouble than you bargained for, I warn you!"

Ramey-Do turned toward his opponents. He swayed languidly back and forth.

"Oh, Karam-Bor! How you *talk*. I mean, why do you want to *badger* them? You know as well as I do that the poor dears have to *eat*. And here you've gone and taken away the only source of food they *have*. And right at their fingertips too. It doesn't make *sense*. They'll *die* if they don't eat. They'll starve away to *nothing*!"

"It's another kind of food they need right now! It's *His* food they want!"

"But you're talking in riddles, dear boy! These two have enough sense to know that the food you can see — see and touch and taste — is ever to be preferred to some...some *figment*! I mean, where *is* this food you're talking about? Where are you *hiding* it? Or are you saying it's invisible? Just can't see it, eh? Oh dear! And how will we ever fill our little tummies? No, my dears," said Ramey-Do, turning back to the youth and the maiden. "Be smart! What do your minds tell you? That this fruit is good to eat. That you have a long journey ahead of you. That you have within your reach all you require to help you to your destination. And remember: the decision is yours alone!"

"Don't listen to him!" Trazel cried out.

But even as his words were spoken, the young woman, trained from infancy as a preparer of food, had plucked one of the fruits. She handed it to the young man. He tore it in two, handing half back to her. Hungrily they devoured it.

"It's as I told you, Trazel," said Karam-Bor wearily. "They're an insufferable, contrary, contumacious breed. Raised to glory one moment, ignorant rebels the next! But ... but it's *your* choice? *Your* favor! Thanks to you, we've made a mistake that will take some doing to set straight!"

The youth and the maiden, meanwhile, had taken to gathering armfuls of fruit to help them with their journey. When they'd gathered as much as they could carry, they set off through the tall grass of the savanna, heading in an easterly direction.

All day long they traveled until, as the sun began to lower, they came to a river. The waters, they could see, thrashed with fish. Tracks leading to the water's edge indicated that here animals came to drink — for them, a ready source of meat. The soil all about them proved to be a rich black loam from which sprang a variety of edible grains and greens and tubers.

Here the two decided to stay. In the days that followed they built a hut to dwell in. They fashioned skins to protect their bodies from the rays of the sun. They learned to strike fire from rock. The young woman experienced the ecstasy of love, but its fruit she bore with screams of agony. The man cherished the solace of his hearthside, with children playing nearby. But these same children grew strong and selfish. And, in their greed, they turned murderous.

Came times when the two would yearn for the simple, uncomplicated existence of the rain forest which had given them life. And so, every now and again they would re-trace their footsteps through oceans of grass toward the wall of the rain forest from which they had emerged.

But as they drew near, they could see the flash of a sword whose blade had been drawn to a fiery keenness, and they came no further. And in time they grew to understand that their past was closed to them forever, and that the way before them lay either upward or nowhere.

"And he placed at the east of the garden of Eden cherubims, and a flaming sword which turned every way, to keep the way of the tree of life."

Genesis 3:24

This book was completed at Bethlehem House, Abbey of the Genesee, on the Feast of the Annunciation, March 25, 1982. It is dedicated to my son, Peter Anders Edman.